rst published in 1916 as *New Battleship Organisations*

is edition published in Great Britain in 2016 by
e Pool of London Press
Division of Casemate Publishers
 Hythe Bridge Street
xford OX1 2EW, UK

ww.pooloflondon.com

The Pool of London Press 2016
troduction © Brian Lavery 2016

CIP record for this book is available from the British Library

rdcover edition: ISBN 978-1-910860-18-2

inted in the Czech Republic by FINIDR s.r.o..

 receive regular email updates on forthcoming Pool of London titles,
ail info@pooloflondon.com with Pool of London Updates in the
ject field.

 a complete list of Pool of London Press and Casemate titles, please contact:
ASEMATE PUBLISHERS (UK)
lephone (01865) 241249
x (01865) 794449
ail: casemate-uk@casematepublishers.co.uk
ww.casematepublishers.co.uk

THE
ROYAL NAVY OFFICER'S
JUTLAND
POCKET-MANUAL 1916

THE
ROYAL NAVY OFFICER'S
JUTLAND
POCKET-MANUAL 1916

First published as

New Battleship Organisations

AND NOTES FOR EXECUTIVE OFFICERS

BEING EXTRACTS FROM A NOTEBOOK, KEPT BY THE
AUTHOR DURING THE LAST FOUR YEARS, ON
NOVEL METHODS OF ORGANISATION, INTERNAL
ECONOMY AND SEAMANSHIP

Commander W.M. James, R.N.

Introduction by Brian Lavery

POOLOFLONDON

The Pool of London Press is a new publisher inspired by the rich history and resonance of the stretch of the River Thames from London Bridge downriver to Greenwich. The Press is dedicated to the specialist fields of naval, maritime, military and exploration history in its many forms. The Press produces beautifully designed, commercial, non-fiction volumes and digital products of outstanding quality for a dedicated readership featuring strong narratives, magnificent illustrations and the finest photography. Recent titles include:

THE LAST BIG GUN
At War & At Sea with HMS *Belfast*
Brian Lavery
£25.00 • Hardback • 376 pages • ISBN: 978-1-910860-01-4

THE COLD WAR SPY POCKET MANUAL
The Official Field-manuals for Spycraft, Espionage and Counter-intelligence
Edited and compiled by Philip Parker
£8.99 • Hardback • 160 pages • ISBN: 978-1-910860-02-1

THE MAPMAKERS' WORLD
A Cultural History of the European World Map
Marjo T. Nurminen
£50.00 • Hardback • 360 pages • ISBN: 978-1-910860-00-7

POOLOFLONDON

www.pooloflondon.com

INTRODUCTION

by Brian Lavery

Some might say that William Milbourne James led a charmed life. His good looks – which he retained all his life – inspired his grandfather Sir John Everett Millais to paint him and it was used as an advertisement for Pears' Soap, which earned his nickname of 'Bubbles'. Even in his fifties an official report described his disposition as 'peculiarly sunny and lovable' and that is reflected in the title of his autobiography *The Sky was Always Blue*. He entered the navy at the age of 13 by the training ship *Britannia* in 1895, and at the beginning of 1913 he gained the vital promotion to commander. He might have become second-in-command of an old cruiser, but instead he was appointed to the battle cruiser *Queen Mary*, building in Palmer's yard on Tyneside and one of the most glamorous ships in the navy. In that post he would be expected to allocate men to the great variety of duties to be done on board.

Admiral 'Jacky' Fisher had shaken up the navy after its long Victorian slumber, reforming the training of officers, recalling ships from imperial policing and scrapping many of the older ones, and building the *Dreadnought*, the prototype for a new class of battleship. But his favourite ship was the battle cruiser, with heavy guns like the battleship, but higher speed and lighter armour – 'eggshells armed with sledgehammers' as he put it. He had intended them to seek out French commerce raiders on the high seas, but now that Germany was the prospective enemy they were to be used as a scouting force for the Dreadnoughts. The *Queen Mary* was the sixth to be built and the third with 13.5 instead of 12-inch guns and a slight improvement on the *Lion* and *Princess Royal* which were just entering service. Like them, the *Queen Mary* had a speed of 27 knots, which demanded huge engines of 75,000 shaft horsepower. Despite plans to change the navy over to oil fuel, they were fed by coal, which demanded an enormous complement of stokers – 526 out of 1017 men on board were in the engineering branch and 471 of these were unskilled or semi-skilled stokers. They could be a problem since they were recruited as adults unlike the seamen who were usually broken into naval discipline as boys, and the great expansion of the navy had led to a lowering of standards. On the other hand, the new First Lord of the Admiralty, Winston Churchill, had given the sailors their first pay rise for half a century and abolished some of the more degrading punishments. Lionel Yexley the lower deck champion hailed it as 'The abolition of discontent' in his newspaper *The Fleet*, but perhaps it was less satisfying to the man on the messdeck.

Captain William Reginald 'Blinker' Hall was appointed to command the ship in July 1913. James had served with him in the cruiser *Natal* and knew him as a brilliant, innovative but difficult officer. Two years ago the Agadir Crisis had convinced almost everyone that war with Germany was highly likely – and indeed the *Queen Mary* herself was part of the arms race which accelerated the process. Therefore Hall told James that 'being certain war was not far off, he wished my peace-time organization for the ship's company to be the same as the organization for war.'[1] This was to be done by dividing the crew into three watches, called red, white and blue instead of the traditional port and starboard, so that the men would get enough rest during constant patrols and sweeps.

Only 250 of the *Queen Mary's* crew were seamen, and 113 of these were trained gunners to operate six 13.5 and 12.4-inch guns (the marines operated the others). Hall's answer was to use stokers to assist the guns' crews when needed, mostly in the magazines. The most radical of Hall's ideas was that the ship was to do without police – the master at arms and ship's corporals. Hall reasoned that petty officers were now of a far higher standard, and that police absolved them from responsibility for the conduct of the ship's company. This was criticised by Yexley, surprisingly since he had written about police corruption in the past.[2] James invited him on board and he was soon full of praise. James does not specifically suggest the absence of police in *New Battleship Organisations*, as other ships still had them, but he by-passes them with his notes on 'Departmental Control of a Ship's Company'.[3] Other innovations included laundries instead of 'dhobying' or washing by hand, a newspaper shop, cinema projector (silent in those days) and a chapel, all of which are described. The section on recreation reflects the fact that seamen no longer got exercise in climbing masts as in the days of sail. The ship carried 3550 tons of coal which had to be stowed by hand as soon as she returned from the sea. William Broadway describes his role. 'Us signal boys used to supply the bags and it did depend on what duty you were on. After coal ship you had to clean up and have a bath and there was absolutely no room as everyone wanted one at the same time. ... your coaling rig you used to bundle up and stow somewhere and then wash it whenever you could.' He was much happier when the ship went to St Petersburg and he looked over the Tsar's palace.[4]

In July 1914 *Queen Mary* sailed from Portland to Scapa Flow and was anchored there when war began on 4 August. She was now part of the Battle Cruiser Force (later Fleet) under the charismatic Rear-Admiral David Beatty and her wartime complement was increased to 1250 men. Hall was transferred to the Naval Intelligence Department in October, where he gained fame in Room 40 at the Admiralty. He was succeeded by Captain Rudolph Bentinck who also 'had the gift of drawing the best out of his officers and men'[5] but soon Captain Cecil Prowse took over. To Beatty he was 'not quite the type of man required for a battle-cruiser, too slow in the brain...'[6] James found him 'of the old-fashioned rigid type.' Prowse hated the Hall system but was unable to change it in view of its obvious efficiency. '... his assumption of command made little difference to the ship's company.'[7] It was perhaps around this time that Trystan Edwards, under training at Portsmouth, discovered that the Queen Mary was 'the happiest ship in the navy' but he was too late to join her.[8]

James left the ship in March 1916 and eventually re-joined Hall in Naval Intelligence. He was in another ship on 31 May when the Queen Mary was third in the line of battle cruisers which steamed into action against the German High Seas Fleet. There was a shock when the Indefatigable at the rear of the line blew up, but the Queen Mary's gunnery seemed to be effective until around 1625 when a flash exploded Q turret's magazine in the centre of the ship, which blew up. It was at this point that Beatty turned to his flag captain Chatfield and remarked. 'There seems to be something wrong with our bloody ships today'.[9] There were only twenty survivors.

The legacy of the ship is to be found in Hall's orders, which became common throughout the fleet and which James describes in this book. Hall went on to become a Conservative MP but sullied his reputation by his involvement in the forged Zinoviev letter which was used to discredit the Labour Government of 1924. James rose through the ranks, published eleven books and became a popular commander-in-chief at Portsmouth in the early stages of the Second World War, flying his flag from Nelson's Victory and still known as 'Bubbles'.

Notes

1. William James, *The Sky was Always Blue*, London, 1951, p. 78.
2. Lionel Yexley, *The Inner Life of the Navy*, London, 1908, passim.
3. *The Sky was Always Blue*, p. 19.
4. Henry Baynham, *Men from the Dreadnoughts*, London, 1976, p. 116, p. 194.
5. *The Sky was Always Blue*, p. 85.
6. Navy Records Society, vol 128, *The Beatty Papers*, Vol 1, ed B McL Ranft, 1989, p. 168.
7. *The Sky was Always Blue*, p. 186.
8. A Trystan Edwards, *Three Rows of Tape*, London, 1929, pp. 19–20.
9. Lord Chatfield, *The Navy and Defence*, London, 1942, p. 143.

Brian Lavery is one of the foremost historians of the Royal Navy. His recent books include *The Last Big Gun: At War and At Sea with HMS* Belfast (2015) *The Mary Rose Manual* (2015), *The Conquest of the Ocean* (2013) and the *Sunday Times* bestseller *Empire of the Seas* (2009).

TO
CAPTAIN W. R. HALL, C.B., R.N.
TO WHOM IS DUE
THE INCEPTION AND INTRODUCTION
INTO H. M. SERVICE
OF MUCH THAT IS IN THIS BOOK

"It is only by judging of results that you will arrive at a just and confident judgment."

—Marquis of Salisbury.

"Certain things are called legitimate because they are old."

—Napoleon.

PREFACE

An old drawing, made in the days of Drake, showing a man taking a range of the enemy by masthead angle and a reference to the importance of using a gunlaying teacher, which can be found in the records of the naval reign of the Earl of St.Vincent, bring home to one the danger of using the word 'novel' in connection with any supposed innovation in H.M. service.

The word 'novel' used on the title page must only be taken to imply that the various odds and ends in this little book are such as have come under the author's notice during the last few years, and are not to be found in other books.

There is no desire to lay down the law; there is no wish to tell naval officers what they ought to do; there is no intention of implying that ships are organised and run on wrong principles.

Instead, there is the hope that naval officers may find something useful in this book, which is a plain account of various schemes which have been successfully carried through in one or more ships during the last few years.

The majority of naval officers would welcome an improvement in the status and command of petty officers, and a return to the days when a man's ship was his home and not a place of business to be left at every opportunity.

Neither are easy to effect: in the first case, because of the cramped life on a man-of-war; in the second case, because naval service is mainly in home waters, with the attendant leave facilities.

But much can be done; and officers, who have these two aims in view, will perhaps find some of these notes of use.

The naval service regards innovations with suspicion until they are well tested, which is natural and right; but there is, unfortunately, a tendency to discover something deleterious to discipline in any scheme which departs from old tradition, however excellent the scheme may be.

Discipline depends on those who command; a form of discipline that is affected unfavourably by a new organisation or the introduction of suitable recreations should be avoided, for it stands self-condemned.

W. M. JAMES,
Commander, R.N.

January 1916.

CONTENTS

LIST OF ILLUSTRATIONS

CHAPTER I

ORGANISING A SHIP'S COMPANY BY NIGHT ATTACK WATCHES

This has come to be known as the 'three-watch' system, which is a misnomer; three watches happens to be the number of watches into which it is possible in many big ships to divide the ship's company for night attack stations.

Some ships can organise an efficient four-watch system and some have only sufficient men for a two-watch system. In the two latter cases no departure is necessary from old-established customs, but many new features arise in the case of a three-watch system, which is the subject of these notes.

If the ship's company are organised into their night attack watches, no change takes place on the declaration of hostilities, commencement of manœuvres, or for the periods of practice firings, and the men are, for all purposes, under the same petty officers and leading seamen and associated with the same topmates.

Naming the Watches.—Difficulty arises in finding suitable titles for these watches. Denominating two watches, starboard and port, had some significance in the days of masts and yards, as each watch worked their own side of the deck when both watches were on deck, but even these names have little connection with the work of a modern ship, except for working the net defence.

There are no suitable nautical terms for denominating three watches, and some simple names that will not clash with other names already in use must be found.

A, B, C lead to confusion with water-tight doors and sea (C) watches. First, second, and third, which have been used for many years in the engine-room department to denominate the three steaming watches, are not satisfactory for general use; such a pipe as 'The second part of the third watch will keep the first watch' would be confusing. Practical, though to many people unpleasant sounding, are three watches known as Red watch, White watch, and Blue watch.

These are distinctive, and become, in a very short time, as natural to everyone on board as port and starboard.

Making out the Watch Bill.—The seamen are divided into three night attack watches.

The marine detachment is divided into three night attack watches.

The engine-room complement is divided into three steaming watches.

The daymen are divided into three watches of equal strength as regards numbers and qualifications.

The following are kept in separate lists and are not detailed by watches:

> Chief petty officers (seamen).
> Quartermasters and boatswains' mates.
> Captain's coxswain.
> Excused daymen.
> Signalmen.

Notes re *Men on Separate Lists.*—1. There is no point in detailing chief petty officers for a watch; they do not work with a watch for ship's work or leave, and, as a rule, are not in a night attack watch.

If a chief petty officer is in a night attack watch, it might seem desirable to put his name in somewhere in that watch, but the watches are necessarily divided into parts of the ship, and he has no connection with a particular part of the ship.

2. Quartermasters and boatswains' mates are usually independent of the night attack watches, and do not work with any watch for ship's work or leave, so are kept on a separate list.

3. Captain's coxswain usually has no watch.

4. With regard to excused daymen, though it is usual to tell the captain's valet, for example, that he belongs to the starboard watch, it is unlikely that he remembers it for long.

5. Signalmen, being organised into daymen and watch-keepers, and not conforming in any way to the routine of the remainder of the ship's company, are placed in a separate list and have their own organisation.

Division into Parts of Ship.—The seamen are divided into those parts of the ship that suit the build of the ship and the armament.

As a rule, ships with three seamen-manned turrets are roughly divided into three equal deck spaces, and therefore require three parts of the ship; similarly, ships with four seamen-manned turrets require four parts of the ship.

There may be ships so constructed and so armed that even five or six parts of the ship may be found the most suitable, so no hard and fast rule can be laid down.

The usual designation for three parts of the ship is forecastle men, top men, and quarter-deck men, but some ships adopt the title 'afterguard' instead of quarter-deck men.

Division into first and second parts is made as usual; further subdivision into subdivisions depends on the strength of the complement.

In most ships it is not possible or necessary; a part of a watch in a three-watch system calls one-sixth of the available seamen for deck duty, and work seldom arises that particularly requires less hands than this part and more than the regular duty hands, i.e. two hands from each part.

Division of Duties.—It is as necessary to divide the various duties equally between the night attack watches as it is when using a two-watch system.

The simplest way to effect this is to make out a table as shown on page 21.

The table is constructed as follows:

All the special duties, boats' crews, etc., are placed as the headings of the columns.

19

Division into three watches is first made, so that the number of 'excused' men is equal for the three watches.

Further division into parts of the ship is then made with the same object in view.

This table having been completed, the special duty and boat columns can then be filled in in the watch bill.

Filling in the Names.—This is entirely dependent on the quarter bill.

The night attack stations are provisionally made out and the watch bill is filled in with as few changes as possible. To merge the two bills together is a matter of 'give and take,' and certain alterations in the night attack stations will be necessary to obtain the right men in the right places for ship's work as well as quarter-bill work.

For example, Horace Needle, A.B., is the most suitable man for sailmaker's mate; he is also a seaman gunner.

In the provisional quarter bill he is shown as a breechworker at a night attack gun in the White watch.

He must be changed with a seaman gunner breechworker in the Red watch in order to assimilate both his duties.

That the watch bill should be entirely interdependent on the quarter bill at first appears rather a large order, but, in practice, there are no difficulties whatsoever.

Division of Engine-room Complement into Parts of Ship.—For all purposes it will be found a good plan to keep the departmental organisation intact for all deck work.

The custom of stationing a whole watch of stokers as one unit for deck work is not sound; they should be detailed by parts of the ship in the same way as the seamen and be controlled by their own petty officers.

They should also fall in always by their parts of the ship, and be ordered by their proper petty officers.

ORGANISATION OF SEAMEN.

(Roman numerals are petty officers and leading seamen.)

	No.	C. Tops and Leading Hands.	Sweepers, &c.	Additional Boys.	P. Boats.	Pinnace.	Launch.	Skiff (or U.D. Sweepers).	Gig (or Spare P.B.).	Galleys.	Whalers.	Cutters (4).	Boatswain's Party.	Torpedo Party.	Torpedo Watch-keepers.	Painting Party.	Side Party.	W.O.'s Servants.	Buglers.	Call Boys.	Side Boys (4), Q.M.'s Mess (2).	Messengers.	Messmen [C.P.O / P.O].	G. L.'s Writer.	Tel. Exchange.	Hold.	Heads.	Sailmaker's Mate.	Bathroom Sweepers.	Boatswain's Yeo.	Armourer's Party.	Turret Sweepers.
Red Watch	66	VI	4		2-II	3	2-I	1	1-I	2	3	19-I	1	7	3	1	2	1	1	1	2	2	2	1	1		1	1	1		1	1
White Watch	67	VII	4		2-I	3	3	1	2	1	2-I	19-II	1	8	3	1	3-I	1	1	1	2	2	3				1		1		1	1
Blue Watch	67	VII	4		2-I	2-I	3	1	2	2	3-I	18-I	1-I	8	2	2	3			2	2	2	3		1	1			1	1		1
	200																															
Fxle Red	23	II	2		1	1	1	1	1	1	1	6-I		2	1			1				1						1				1
White	22	II	1		1-I	1	1		1	1	1	6		2	1		1			1		1	1				1				1	
Blue	22	II	1		1	1	1		1		1	6-I		2	1	1	1	1			1	1	1		1				1	1		
Top Red	22	II	1		1-I	1	1	1		1	1-I	6	1	3	1	1	1-I		1				1				1		1			1
White	22	II	1		1	1	1				1	6-I		3	1		1	1			1		1									
Blue	22	III	2		1	1	1		1	1	1	6		3	1		1			1	1		1		1	1						
Q.D. Red	22	II	1		1	1	1		1		1	7		2	1		1			1	1	1	1	1							1	
White	22	III	1			1	1		1			7-I		3	1	1	1		1		1	1	1						1			
Blue	23	II	2		1	1	1	1		1	1-I	6	1-I	3		1	1			1		1	1									1
	200																															

In a battle cruiser these parts are:
    A Boiler room.
    B Boiler room.
    C Boiler room.
    D Boiler room.
    E Boiler room.
    F Boiler room.
    G Boiler room.
    Forward engine room.
    After engine room.
(See 'Parades' and 'Stationing.')

Duty Watch.—*Sea.*—The night attack watches and steaming watches take watch on deck and watch below respectively in regular rotation, i.e. Red, White, Blue, Red, White, Blue *et seq.*

Proceeding to Sea.—The duty watch on board completes the watch during which the ship sails, the other watches following in rotation.

Harbour.—The watches take duty watch in rotation from noon to the following noon.

Stand-by Watch.—The stand-by watch is always the next duty watch.

Leave.—*Home Ports.*—Leave can be given to two watches every night, thus keeping a complete night attack and steaming watch on board.

Foreign Ports.—Leave as a rule to one watch each day.

Home Dockyard (alongside).—Leave as a rule to two watches and a part of the third watch.

Notes on this Leave.—Home ports are the ship's depot port and Portland for a home fleet battleship. It depends, of course, on the usual anchorage.

More men do not go on leave each night than with a watch and watch system; the men have more choice of days to go ashore, but they are not so overburdened with pocket-money that they can take advantage of every day leave is piped.

As a rule at foreign ports, leave to one watch is as much as can be given with the available boats; this leave is not much sought after by the lower deck, most men like one run ashore at a foreign port and are not keen to go again.

In order to vary the week-end leave at home ports, the same watch takes duty for two days running—namely, Wednesday and Thursday.

The leave for a week is as follows:

Day	Duty Watch	Leave for
Saturday	Blue	Red, White
Sunday	Red	White, Blue
Monday	White	Blue, Red
Tuesday	Blue	Red, White
Wednesday	Blue	Red, White
Thursday	Red	White, Blue
Friday	White	Blue, Red

The duty watch of the previous twenty-four hours is always the 'major' watch for leave, and this watch proceeds on leave if leave is to only one watch or the work of the ship requires two watches on board to a time after the leave commences.

Should it be necessary to bring the leave into line with a ship that is working in two watches, this is done by piping leave to a watch and a part of the 'stand-by' watch, the part depending, as usual, on the day of the month.

Dockyard port leave. The part of the duty watch proceeds on leave after the work of the day is completely finished.

CHAPTER II

ORGANISATION BY ARMAMENT

The division of a sailing ship's complement into four parts of the ship—namely, forecastle men, foretop men, maintop men, and mizentop men (or quarter-deck men)—has been retained in modern ships because four parts, as a rule, suited the build and armament, and two of the four names still express the sections of the ship where the seamen work, i.e. forecastle and quarter-deck.

Battle cruisers (with all turrets on the centre line) are the first big ships whose build and armament make it undesirable to divide the complement into four parts; the upper deck is built in three nearly equal sections—namely, fxle and fore 4″ battery, waist, after 4″ battery and quarter-deck, and there is one seaman-manned turret on each deck.

In these ships, therefore, three parts of the ship have been adopted, and these are named forecastle men, top men, and quarterdeck men (or afterguard).

This is only a slight variation from the established custom, but the build and armament of some ships recently commissioned, and probably of new ships designed or building, are making, and will in the future make it more and more difficult to retain the old-fashioned organisation, and it is possible that an entirely new organisation by armament, which will suit every type of ship, will be found the most suitable.

By 'organisation by armament' is meant the organisation of the ship's company by their action stations for all purposes. There are no parts of the ship as generally understood; instead, a man, for example, who is stationed for action in A turret, is one of 'A turret's crew' for cleaning ship, stationing, messing, and general ship's work.

The following notes are made for a battle cruiser, but the same principle can be applied to any ship.

Parts of the Ship.—
    A Turret. (Marines.)
    B Turret.
    Q Turret.
    X Turret.
    4″ Battery. (Day action gun and magazine crews.)
    Middle-deck men. (Transmitting station crew, working party, control-tower crews, etc.)
    Torpedo.
These parts are nearly equal in strength.

Division into Parts.—If desired, the subdivision into a first and a second part can be easily made as follows:
Turrets:
    First part.—Gunhouse and working-chamber crew.
    Second part.—Magazine and shell-room crews.
4″ Battery:
    First part.—The foremost half of the guns each side and the fore magazine crew.
    Second part.—The after half of the guns each side land the after magazine crew.
Torpedo:
    Divided arbitrarily.
Middle-deck men:
    Divided arbitrarily.

Division into Watches.—This is done as usual into the night attack watches.

Those men who are not in a night attack watch are arbitrarily placed in a watch for ship's duties.

Watch Bill.—The only bill required in the ship is, therefore, a combined watch, night attack, and day action bill.

There are no particular difficulties in making out the bill; it is an expansion of the night attack watch bill previously described.

The engine-room complement are in any case organised by their action stations, i.e. their boiler and engine rooms.

Officers of Divisions.—The officers of turrets are in command of their own crews.

The officer of day action crews is in command of the 4″ battery.

The officer in charge of the transmitting station is in command of the middle-deck men.

The torpedo officer commands his own men.

Petty Officers of Divisions.—There may be a shortage of petty officers in the case of the middle-deck men, but as the messengers, side boys, call boys, etc., come out of this part of the ship, it can be made a leading seaman's command.

Cleaning Ship.—Upper deck:

A Turret (marines).—Flats, officers'
    messes.
B Turret.—Forecastle.
Q Turret.—Waist.
X Turret.—Quarter deck.
4″ Battery.—4″ batteries.
Middle-deck men.—Shelter decks and boat decks.

Mess deck:

Each division messes together as far as possible. The sweepers
    for each mess deck are supplied by the division of the deck.

Division of Duties.—The division of special duties and boats equally between all parts and watches, as previously described for a three-night attack watch bill, is again necessary, but in this case it cannot be applied to all duties.

The following are some of the exceptions;

(1) Boat duties cannot be taken by torpedo division, except when called away 'for exercise.'

(2) Call boys, side boys, messengers, and buglers all come out of the middle-deck men.

(3) The middle-deck men will not contain many able seamen, and therefore such an accurate division of 'excused duties' will be impossible.

Coaling.—No. 1 Hold, B Turret and 4″ Battery.

No. 2 Hold, Q Turret and middle-deck men.

No. 3 Hold, X Turret and torpedo division.

No. 4 Hold, A Turret and remainder of detachment.

Stationing the Ship's Company.—It will be found that in nearly all stations six tasks of about equal work can be found.

As an example a portion of a station bill is given on p. 28.

—		Entering Harbour	Watch (a) Out mat. (b) Main derrick.
B Turret.	Red. White Blue.	Fxle. Fxle. Main derrick.	(a) Bottom line. (b) Port fore guy.
Q Turret.	Red. White Blue.	Lower booms. Waist ladder. Main derrick.	(a) Mat. (b) Starbd. after guy.
X Turret.	Red. White Blue.	Quarter booms. Ladders. Main derrick.	(a) Aft fore and after. (b) Port aft guy.
4″ Battery.	Red. White Blue.	Starbd. small derrick. Main derrick.	(a) Diving pump. (b) Starbd. aft guy.
Middle- deck men.	Red. White Blue.	Port small derrick. Main derrick.	(a) Fore fore and after. (b) Boat ropes and stern fasts.
A Turret. (Marines).	Red. White Blue.	Port aft guy, boom. Starbd. aft guy, boom. Waist ladder.	(a) Assist with mat. (b) Steadying lines.

Stokers and daymen as described in the 'night attack watch' station bill on pp. 48, 49.

CHAPTER III

DEPARTMENTAL CONTROL OF A SHIP'S COMPANY

'**D**epartmental control' means the supervising of each branch of the ship's company by its own petty officers for all purposes.

The usual custom is for the marine detachment to be entirely supervised by its non-commissioned officers, but the seaman branch and engine-room complement to be supervised by a staff of ship's police for certain matters of regulation and discipline.

Practically all that is done is to place the different departments under the same regulation as the marine detachment.

Departments.—The four departments in a ship are:

Seamen (includes daymen, excused daymen, and electrical artificers).

Engine-room department (except engine-room artificers).

Marine detachment.

Engine-room artificers.

The engine-room artificers are made a separate department, as the senior artificer on board is usually senior to the senior representative of the other departments.

Staff.—Seaman branch:

    One chief petty officer.

    One boatswain's mate to each mess deck.

Engine-room department:

    One chief stoker.

    Stoker petty officers as chief stoker's mates in proportion to complement.

(One per hundred of complement has been found about the right number.)

Marine detachment:
   One serjeant-major.
   N.C.O.'s as detailed.

Engine-room artificers:
   Senior engine-room artificer.

Duties.—To superintend the mess deck, superintend the leave, parade and muster defaulters, and keep the books.

The staff for seaman branch are also detailed for stations for drills and evolutions, for action and night attack stations, and, as circumstances may require, for such ship's work as should be performed by a seaman petty officer.

The staff for stoker branch are employed when necessary, e.g. full-speed steaming.

Titles.—It is an advantage to designate these ratings by a special title, and the following have been found sufficiently distinctive:

Seamen.—The chief petty officer and boatswain's mates of the mess deck.

Engine-room department.—The chief stoker and chief stoker's mates.

An alternative, which avoids confusion with the chief stoker of the mess deck, is to call the chief stoker the 'master stoker' and his mates 'master stoker's mates.'

Interchange of Duties.—The chief boatswain's mate of the mess deck should be able at any time to take the duties of the chief petty officer.

The chief stoker of the mess deck should at any time be able to take the duties of the master or chief stoker.

The senior N.C.O. always does take the duties of serjeant-major when the latter is absent from sickness or other cause.

Staff not to be Permanent.—The duties performed by the boatswain's mates of the mess deck and the chief stoker's mates do not require specialisation, and can be performed by any petty officer fit to hold that rating.

These petty officers should be relieved as often as circumstances permit; unless there is a special reason, a petty officer should not be retained on this staff for longer than six months.

This cannot be applied to the chief petty officer, chief stoker, and chief E.R.A., as they, of necessity, should be the senior suitable man in each case.

Regulating.—The chief petty officer, chief stoker, serjeant-major, and chief E.R.A. keep their respective departmental watch bills.

They also tell off all working parties, special parties, pickets, etc.

Note.—As a variation of this, it has been found a good working scheme for the chief boatswain's mate of the mess deck to carry out all detailing of parties and pickets, as he has not a great deal of work to do once the ship is settled down.

Superintending the Mess Deck.—The boatswain's mates, chief stoker's mates, N.C.O.'s, and chief E.R.A. are severally responsible for the cleanliness and order of their own decks and messes.

Superintending the Leave.—When liberty men fall in, they fall in by their separate departments. They are paraded, checked, and reported for inspection to the inspecting officer by the senior duty boatswain's mate, chief stoker's mate, or N.C.O. They are then marched to the boat or gangway by these departmental petty officers.

When liberty men return from leave, they are received at the gangway by the senior duty boatswain's mate, chief stoker's mate, or N.C.O. They are searched, paraded, checked, and reported for inspection to the inspecting officer by these departmental petty officers.

Parading of Defaulters.—*General.*—Men holding the rating of petty officer or above are always paraded by the chief petty officer, chief stoker, serjeant-major, or chief E.R.A.

Men holding ratings below that of petty officer are paraded by boatswain's mates, chief stoker's mates, and N.C.O.'s.

The only exception to this is at captain's defaulters *(q.v)*.

Officer of the Watch or Day's Defaulters.—When it is required to bring a defaulter before the officer of the day, the duty boatswain's mate, duty chief stoker's mate, or duty N.C.O. parade him, if below the rank of petty officer.

The officer's decision is entered in the proper book and the entry is transferred to the Commander's Defaulters' Book if so ordered.

The chief petty officer, chief stoker, serjeant-major, or chief E.R.A. are always to be sent for if the defaulter is of or above the rank of petty officer.

Commander's Defaulters.—The chief petty officer, chief stoker, serjeant-major, and chief E.R.A. are responsible for the parading of the defaulters at the ordered time.

Each department prepares Form S 241 for their own defaulters. This form is placed before the commander as each defaulter is reported, and he enters his decision on the form under the offender's name.

Should he decide to forward the case for the captain's decision, he writes 'Captain' under the defaulter's name, and the *same* form is kept and presented to the captain at captain's defaulters.

The chief petty officer, chief stoker, serjeant-major, and chief E.R.A. in the case of petty officers and above, and the senior boatswain's mate and senior chief stoker's mate in the case of men below the rank of petty officer, enter the commander's decision in the proper book.

Commander's Request Men.—Separate books are kept in each department for petty officers and men below that rank, and they are paraded in the same manner as the defaulters.

Captain's Defaulters and Request Men.—Form S 241 as it left the commander is presented to the captain. His decision is entered below the defaulter's name and also entered in the proper book.

All captain's defaulters and request men are paraded by the chief petty officer, chief stoker, serjeant-major, or chief E.R.A.

Form S 241.—It will be observed that this form is used throughout. By this means no mistakes can possibly creep in.

The forms are taken after commander's or captain's defaulters direct to the captain's office, where they are filed and taken charge of by the captain's clerk, who keeps the conduct books and daily record.

Carrying out of Punishments.—At the regulation times, the duty boatswain's mate, duty chief stoker's mate, and N.C.O. parade and report the men under punishment as present or not present to the officer of the watch or day.

If extra work is ordered, the O.O.W. or O.O.D. orders the work to be done.

If drill is ordered, the men under punishment are squadded together and taken charge of by the drill instructor.

A duty leading seaman, leading stoker, or N.C.O. is detailed daily to be present and supervise the extra work under the duty boatswain's mate, chief stoker's mate, or serjeant.

Drill instructors are chosen from those petty officers and N.C.O.'s who are specially proficient at drill, in order that the drill can be well carried out, e.g. gunner's mates, serjeants, and selected petty officers, whose duties admit of this work.

Mails.—A selected boatswain's mate and chief stoker's mate superintend the distribution of the mails.

Messing.—All these C.P.O.'s and P.O.'s mess in their proper messes.

Keeping the Books.—The prevalent idea that keeping the books requires a specialised staff is an erroneous one. There is nothing that any man fit to hold the rating of petty officer cannot easily do.

The following books are kept by each department:

Books	Kept by
1. Captain's Request Book.	C.P.O., chief stoker, serjeant-major, and C.E.R.A.
2. Captain's Defaulters' Book.	
3. Commander's Defaulter's Book.	Senior boatswain's mate, senior chief stoker's mate, serjeant-major, and C.E.R.A.
4. Commander's Request Book.	
5. Night Round's Book.	Supervised by C.P.O.
6. Gangway Wine and Spirit Book.	Selected boatswain's mate.
7. Gangway Victualling and Check Book.	Senior boatswain's mate, senior chief stoker's mate, and serjeant-major (see footnote).
8. Rum Stoppage.	Selected boatswain's mate, selected chief stoker's mate, and serjeant-major.
9. Short-leave Book.	Duty boatswain's mate, duty chief stoker's mate, duty N.C.O., and duty E.R.A.

Books	Kept by
10. Mess Book.	Senior boatswain's mate, senior chief stoker's mate, serjeant-major, and C.E.R.A.
11. Register Letter and Parcel Book.	Selected boatswain's mate.
12. Address Book.	Selected boatswain's mate, selected chief stoker's mate, serjeant-major, and C.E.R.A.

Notes.—In order to minimise number of books, chief stoker keeps Nos. 7 and 8 for the engine-room artificer branch.

A boatswain's mate is shown as keeping Nos. 6 and 11, but a chief stoker's mate could equally well be detailed if necessary.

Captain's clerk keeps daily record.

Rounds.—The duty boatswain's mate, duty chief stoker's mate, and senior N.C.O. attend commanding officer's rounds, each submitting the rounds' report of his own department.

The chief petty officer, or one of the boatswain's mates, is responsible for the locking up of officers' messes.

Escorts.—Always provided from the same department as the offender belongs to.

Note.—It is customary to employ marines for this duty, but two marines are in no respect more suitable for taking charge of an able seaman than are two able seamen.

Sentry on Prisoners.—Provided always by the department to which the prisoner belongs. Cell prisoners are under the charge of the chief petty officer, chief stoker, or serjeant-major as the case may be.

General Note.—The foregoing orders may at first sight appear rather complicated, but all that is really done is to place the seamen, stokers, and E.R.A.'s on exactly the same footing as the marine detachment are for all purposes, petty officers being detailed specially for certain books.

The order *re* petty officers and chief petty officers only being dealt with by chief petty officers, is very necessary in view of the status and position in the ship of chief petty and petty officers.

The whole system has in actual practice worked excellently.

CHAPTER IV

DIVISIONAL CONTROL OF SHIP'S COMPANY

Adisadvantage of the departmental control described in the previous chapter is that the seamen still come under two lots of petty officers, i.e. the captains of tops on deck and the boatswain's mates below.

The petty officers, therefore, do not obtain that full control of their men which is so necessary if their position and status in the ship is to be kept at a high standard.

The following system of divisional control has worked well in one of H.M. ships.

Officer of Division.—Is responsible for all decks and flats that are looked after and cleaned by his men.

He sees all request men at divisions.

Chief Captain of Top.—Takes a similar position to a marine senior N.C.O. in a man-of-war.

He acts as the officer of division's right-hand man in all matters connected with the division.

He collects all requests from the division and parades the request men for the officer of division.

He is responsible that one of the captains of tops of his division is always detailed for the 'special duties' enumerated below.

He is in charge of all gear belonging to his top and is responsible that all pipes affecting his top as a whole are obeyed.

For example, the order to 'Secure nets for sea' is piped; each watch secure their own sections, but the chief captain of top inspects the work on completion and reports the nets secured to the C.O. or O.O.D. He takes the reports from the captains of top when the hands are fallen in. At telling off the hands, when it is immaterial which watch a man comes from, the chief captain of top details him from one of his watches according to circumstances—e.g., commander orders 'one hand from each part of the ship for the ship's steward'; as it is immaterial to the commander which particular watch supplies these men, chief captains of tops each detail one man from one of their watches.

He is in general charge of his section of the deck and is responsible for its cleanliness.

At evolutions, clean ship, etc., it is his duty, in the event of some part of the men under his command being absent, to arrange for all the work being carried out—e.g. a watch is away from 'scrub decks'; he will arrange that the other watch or two watches scrub the absent men's part. (With a two-watch system it is, of course, perfectly obvious that the remaining watch must scrub the whole deck; but with a three-watch system and a large deck, the chief captain of top has constantly to rearrange his watches.)

The chief captains of tops are detailed to work with a complete watch of seamen, one to each watch. When a watch falls in, the chief captain of top musters and reports to the officer in charge and assists him in carrying out the work.

A senior petty officer or chief petty officer is detailed for chief captain of top.

Captains of Top.—A captain of top is detailed for each watch as usual.

One of these petty officers is told off as the 'special duty captain of top.' These petty officers take this duty in turn.

Captain of Top for Special Duties.—This petty officer's special duty is the supervision of the division's mess deck.

He takes command of his men on all occasions, but at such times as the mess deck is being cleaned or cleared up, he supervises the work and turns the command of the men on deck over to his leading seaman.

He parades the request men and defaulters of his own division at the routine times under the direction of the chief petty officer of the ship.

In practice, this petty officer is only away from his men for short periods; he is always present at all parades for inspection or telling-off, and if his men are employed on important work during mess-deck cleaning hours, he remains in command of them.

The chief captain of top should always keep an eye on this petty officer's watch when he is carrying out his special duties.

Clearing up Decks for Night Rounds.—Captains of tops of watch on deck take this duty in turn and stand the rounds on their respective decks.

Locking up Officers' Messes and First Watch Rounds.— The captains of tops for special duty take this duty in turn.

Parading Men under Punishment.—Captains of tops for special duty take this duty in turn, and after reporting 'present' to the officer of the day, put them to work under the duty leading seaman or turn them over to the duty drill instructor.

Interchange of Duties.—One of the other captains of same top will always be detailed to take the duties of the captain of top for special duty if the latter is on leave or employed with his own men at times when a petty officer for his special duties is required.

Artisans, Torpedo Party, etc.—*Artisans.*—The chief shipwright is responsible for the parading of artisan request men and defaulters.

Torpedo Party.—A selected torpedo petty officer is responsible for the torpedo party.

Armourers.—The chief armourer is responsible for the armourers.

Signalmen.—The chief yeoman or senior yeoman is responsible for the signalmen.

Mail Petty Officer.—The mails and cells are the two duties that were formerly taken by the ship's police which are not suitable duties for a captain of top, and a petty officer, termed the mail petty officer, is detailed for these duties.

This petty officer takes his turn with the special duty captains of tops for locking up messes, night rounds, and parading men under punishment.

He also is responsible for the parading of defaulters and request men not previously mentioned—e.g. cook ratings, ship's steward, and writer ratings.

Note.—The captains of tops for special duty necessarily have more duties to perform than the other captains of tops.

As a rule the captain of top who took the previous night duty should be permitted to stand off during the afternoon.

In any case, the captains of tops frequently change rounds.

Books.—The captains of tops for special duty keep the books instead of the boatswain's mates as described in Chapter IV.

E.R. Department.—Are organised on exactly the same lines as described in Chapter IV.

Clear Lower Deck.—At the pipe for 'clear lower deck' the captains of tops for special duty clear their respective decks.

With regard to the ordinary watch bugles and pipes, the responsibility of the men being present rests with the petty officers of parts of ship.

If it is understood that a petty officer reporting his men present when they are not is guilty of a serious offence, the necessity of having one lot of petty officers chasing up men from the mess deck, and one lot waiting for them on deck, will disappear.

If a bugle is sounded for a company of soldiers to fall in, N.C.O.'s chasing men out of the barrack rooms is not part of the procedure; instead, the N.C.O.'s are relied on to report any absentees.

Mess Deck Patrol.—The captains of tops for special duty patrol their mess decks at odd times during the day to see everything is in order.

Note.—This organisation can be made a great success if fully explained to all officers and petty officers and provided the co-operation of all the officers is obtained.

In the ship where this organisation is working, the chief captains of tops not only act as C.P.O. of division and deck, but are also frequently given command of a watch when officers are not available. For example, torpedoes have just been picked up and are returning to ship in tow of cutter and whaler and the ship is coming to single anchor:—

Chief Captain of Fxle.—Hoists in cutter with Red watch.

Chief Captain of Top.—Hoists in whaler with White watch.

Chief Captain of Quarter-deck.—Gets out quarter-booms with Blue watch.

Occasions are frequent during practices when there are not enough officers to 'go round,' and it is quite wrong and unnecessary for each operation to be done piecemeal so that an officer can be present.

Some officers will, perhaps, to put it mildly, raise their eyebrows at the suggestion that a petty officer should hoist in a cutter by derrick; but they can and do do it, and their position and status in the ship are enhanced in consequence.

NOTE ON CHAPTERS I–IV

Chapter I deals with a new watch system, Chapter II deals with a new part of the ship system, Chapters III and IV deal with new systems of command. The system described in Chapter IV is a variation of that part of Chapter III which deals with the seamen branch, and experience has shown it to be an improvement.

Should it be desired to adopt these new organisations in a man-of-war, the following will be the procedure:

1. Make division into 'parts of ship' by the armament and name them accordingly.

2. Tell off 'clean ship' stations for the 'parts of the ship,' keeping the men as closely associated with their guns, etc., as possible.

3. Make out a station bill as far as possible in accordance with the position of the armament—e.g. foremost turret's crew do cable work.

4. Having settled on the number of watches into which the ship's company can efficiently be divided for night attack, divide the ship's company into that number.

5. Make a natural division into 'parts of watches' as far as possible—e.g. gun-house and working-chamber crew are about equal in strength to the remainder of a turret's crew.

6. As soon as the gunnery and torpedo officers' bills are ready, hold a meeting and fill in the watch bill, adjusting so that each man's various duties are assimilated.

7. Make out orders for the command of the seaman branch in accordance with Chapter IV, detailing leading seamen to take charge of watches where necessary—e.g. watches of middle-deck men and certain watches of the other 'parts of ship' will probably be leading seamen's commands, as there will not be sufficient petty officers for all the commands; so much the better, it will give them a chance of command they seldom get.

8. Make out orders for the command of the engine-room department in accordance with Chapter III.

CHAPTER V

DECENTRALISATION OF COMMAND

Ships vary enormously in the matter of decentralisation.

A few years back it was almost the universal custom for everything to be centralised in the hands of the executive officer.

Not even the skiff could be called away in some ships without reference to him.

There are a large number of officers and petty officers in a man-of-war, and the *real defect of this centralisation is that it deprives them of initiative and chances of exercising command and judgment.*

The great difficulty that faces an executive officer who believes in decentralisation is one of fixing limits, and when he has fixed these, he is again anxious about the ability of those under his command to carry through successfully the work required.

Nothing in these notes must be taken as meaning that there is no supervision by a senior officer; a senior officer must supervise in the early days of a commission, but, if he wishes to successfully decentralise, he must confine himself to watching and correcting mistakes. The lieutenant, warrant officer, midshipman, or petty officer actually in command must give the orders.

The self-confidence and power of command that these officers and petty officers acquire in a very short time, if given a chance, is great.

Stationing.—The stationing of the ship's company is an admirable opportunity for decentralising.

Station bills have been made out to such detail as, for example, 'Nos. 114, 115, 116 provide block and strop.' If No. 114 is in cells and No. 115 is on the sick list, No. 116, who perhaps is a minute boy, finds himself confronted by a Herculean task.

The stations issued by the executive officer should be as brief as possible and contain no unnecessary detail.

The detail is to be made out by the officers in charge or the petty officers.

A station bill on these lines is given on pp. 46–9, and the following two examples will show what should be done by the officers and petty officers:

(1) *Station 'Out bower anchor.'*—Fxle men Red watch are detailed for 'work cables'; top men Red watch to assist them.

The first lieutenant, either before or when the ship's company are stationed for this drill for the first time, explains what has to be done by the fxle men and the top men, and tells the captains of these two tops the number of men he requires for each separate job—i.e. the pendant, the blacksmith's work, the mooring pendant, etc.

The captains of tops detail the leading hands and the men in their part of the ship in accordance with the first lieutenant's orders.

(2) *Watch 'Out hedge anchor.'*—Fxle men are detailed for 'anchor and lowering tackle' (in this particular case the anchor was stowed close to a cutter's davit).

Top men are detailed for '5″ and lower cutter.'

Quarter-deck men are detailed for 'Luffs, strops, buoy, buoy rope, mat.'

The captains of the fxle detail in their own books men to provide the tackle, men to cast off the lashings, and men to stock the anchor if necessary.

The captains of the top detail in their own books men for the foremost fall, men for the afterfall, and men for the 5″ hawser.

The captains of the quarter-deck detail in their own books men for each of the items they are responsible for providing.

This all sounds very simple, but it will be found to require a great deal of self-denial if it is to be a success.

The commander must content himself with these very brief stations, and officers in charge of the different operations must be content to describe the work to be done and the number of men required, and leave the captains of tops to tell off the men.

It will be noticed that the stokers are detailed by their 'parts of the ship.' They thus work under their proper petty officers, have a job of their own to do instead of being 'massed' for every evolution, and the evolution is independent of the number of watches of stokers on deck ; this latter is an important point, as stations that depend on, say, two watches of stokers for their successful performance, are likely to come to grief one day, whereas variation in the numbers available for a particular job is the only effect of altering the number of watches in the system recommended.

		Entering Harbour	In and out Nets (Bullivant system)	Bower anchor	Sheet anchor and weigh by hand	Stern anchor	Tow forward
Pipes		'Prepare for entering harbour' 'Fall in for entering harbour' Bugle 'Advance'—man guys, etc. Bugle 'G'—haul forward, lower away, top derricks, lower boats, spread awnings	'Out nets.' 'G'—'Roll over' 'Advance'—Haul forward 'In nets' 'G'—'Let go haul aft' Advance—'Commence roll'	'Out bower anchor' 'Away launch and pinnace for exercise. Away—cutter'	'Weigh by hand'	'Out stream anchor' 'Away launches for exercise'	'Prepare to tow forward' 'Away 1st and 2nd seaboats'
F.X.	Red	Fxle	Fore working guys	Work cables	Work cables	Assist quarter-deck men	Cables
	White	Fxle Stump derricks	Boom men (Booms 1–6)	Grass line and stern fast for launch	Work cables	Ditto	5½" wire Heaving line
	Blue	Main derrick	Brail men	Main derrick Then 6½"	Clear away in wake of capstan	Main derrick	6½" wire Heaving line
Top	Red	Lower booms	Auxiliary working guys	Tail jiggers, etc., in launch; assist Red fxle		4½" wire in boat	Easing out gear for 6½"
	White	Stump derrick Lower cutter	Boom men (Booms 7–12)	Grass line and stern fast for pinnace	Fall in abaft breakwater till required	4½" wire in boat	Lower boats
	Blue	Main derrick	Brail men	Main derrick Then 6½"		Main derrick	Easing out gear for 5½"
Q.D.	Red	Quarter and stern booms	After working guys	Kedge	Capstan bars and rig capstan, pay down cable	Ship rollers, provide pendant; bring to capstan	6" Manilla
	White	Accom. ladder Stump derrick	Boom men (Booms 13–18)	Kedge			5" Manilla
	Blue	Main derrick	Brail men	Main derrick Then 6½"		Main derrick, then mat, buoy and buoy rope	Grass lines to cutters
Marines	Red	Waist ladder if inboard Then starbd. guy. Lower boom		6½"			6½"
	White	Waist ladder if inboard Then port guy, Lower boom	Bearing out spars for 'out nets' Hand brails for 'in nets'	6½"	Fall in abaft breakwater till required	Fall in	6½"
	Blue	Waist ladder if inboard Then starbd. or port guy Lower boom		6½"			5½"

BILL

Tow aft	Fire. General	Clear for action	Out wire hawsers	Collision	Away all boats	Watch (a) Kedge anchor (b) Fire engines (c) Diving boat (d) Collision mat (e) Stump derrick
'Prepare to tow aft' 'Seaboats crews fall in'	'Fire bell' 'Still.' 'Fire at—'		'Out all wire hawsers' 'Away launches and pinnaces for exercise, 1st and 2nd cutters'	'Foghorn rapid blasts' 'Still' 'Place of collision named'	'Away all boat's crews'	(a) 'Watch out kedge. 'Away 1st and 2nd cutters' (b) 'Watch out fire engines' 'Away 1st and 2nd cutters and whaler' (c) 'Watch rig diving boat Away—' (d) 'Watch place collision mat at—' (e) 'Watch work starbd. or port small derrick' 'Out—'
Starboard towing slip Port towing slip Fall in ready for hauling	Fire Ventilation Then stump derrick Main derrick	Jackstaff(and signalmen) Down all stanchions, guardrails,etc.	6½" 5½" Main derrick Then 6½"		Starbd. small derrick Port small derrick Main derrick	(a) Anchor and lowering tackle (b) In boats (c) Pump (d) Bottom line, foremost fore and after (e) Topping lift and bow lines
3" luff and stopper Lower boats 2" luff and stopper	Fire Ventilation Then stump derrick Main derrick	In cutters In cutters In cutters	6½" Lower cutters Then 5½" Main derrick Then 5½"	Watch on deck—Close W. T. doors Stand-by watch—Out mat! Second stand-by watch— Prepare derricks'	Starbd. small derrick Port small derrick Main derrick	(a) 5" and lower cutter (b) Engines and hoses (c) Dresses, boots, helmets, weights, breastropes, telephone (d) Mat (e) Inboard guy and stern lines
Grass hawser, port Grass hawser, starbd. Clear away rails, etc.	Fire Ventilation Then stump derrick Main derrick	Ensign staff (and signalmen) Port accom. ladders Starbd. accom. ladders	4½" 3½" Main derrick Then 6½"		Starbd. small derrick Port small derrick Main derrick	(a) Luffs, strops, buoy, buoy rope and mat (b) Grapnels, buckets (c) Shot rope, distance line, ladder (d) Pump and after fore and after (e) Forward outboard guy and purchase
Fall in	Fall in	Waist accommodation ladder	6½" 5½" 6½"			(a) Assist with anchor (b) Assist with engines, provide guard (c) Six lengths of air piping (d) Mat (e) After outboard guy

—	—	Entering Harbour	In and out Nets (Bullivant system)	Bower anchor	Sheet anchor and weigh by hand	Stern anchor	Tow forward
Stokers	'A' Boil. room	Assist with wires on fxle	Working guys port waist	6½"	'Fall in in usual positions until ordered to man bars as requisite	Not required	6½"
	'B' Boil. room	Bearing out spar. Starbd. lower boom	Working guys starbd. waist	6½"			6½"
	'C' Boil. room	Bearing out spar. Port lower boom	Working guys port waist	6½"			6½"
	'D' Boil. room	Starbd. boom guy. Port fore M. Dk. guy if working by hand	Working guys starbd. waist	Starbd. fore main derrick guy if working by hand —then 6½"			6½"
	'E' Boil. room	Port boom guy. Port fore M. Dk. guy if working by hand	Working guys port waist	Port fore main derrick guy if working by hand —then 6½"			5½"
	'F' Boil. room	Starbd. fore M. Dk. guy if working by hand; waist awning	Working guys starbd. waist	Starbd. fore main derrick guy if working by hand —then 6½"			5½"
	'G' Boil. room	Starbd. after M. Dk. guy if working by hand; waist awning	Working guys starbd. waist	Starbd. after main derrick guy if working by hand —then 6½"			5½"
	' Fore E.R.'	Port after M. Dk. guy if working by hand; waist awning	Working guys port waist	Port after main derrick guy if working by hand —then 6½"			5½"
	' Aft. E.R.'	Port after M. Dk. guy if working by hand; waist awning	Working guys port waist	Port after main derrick guy if working by hand —then 6½"			5½"
Daymen		Cable. Cable holders. Ladders	Attend sections as detailed by carpenter	Cable holders. In boats as detailed	Swifter	Blacksmith for shackling on	Blacksmith for cables Cable holders
Notes		Derrick guys usually worked by motor; stokers detailed for guys, then prepare waist awnings for spreading					Seaboats lowered if necessary

Tow aft	Fire.	General	Clear for action	Out wire hawsers	Collision	Away all boats	Watch (a) Kedge anchor (b) Fire engines (c) Diving boat (d) Collision mat (e) Stump derrick
Fall in in usual positions until required for hauling in				6½″ 6½″ 6½″ Starbd. fore main derrick guy if working by hand— then 6½ Port fore main derrick guy if working by hand —then 5½″ Starbd. fore main derrick guy if working by hand— then 5½″ Starbd. after main derrick guy if working by hand —then 5½″ Port after main derrick guy if working by hand —then 5½″ Port after main derrick guy if working by hand —then 5½″		Port small derrick guys Starbd. small derrick guys Port small derrick guys Starbd. fore main derrick guys if worked by hand Port fore main derrick guy if worked by hand Starbd. fore main derrick guy if worked by hand Starbd. after main derrick guy if worked by hand Port after main derrick guy if worked by hand Port after main derrick guy if worked by hand	
Blacksmiths Stoppers Seaboats lowered if necessary	At fire under ch. carp.	Attend sections as detailed by carpenter		6½″ Launch 5½″ Pinnace 4½″ Cutter 3½″ Cutter	Fall in ready to work under carpenter		

Decentralisation for Officers.—*Operations performed by 'hands' or more than one watch.*—For 'hands' operations the executive officer should be in command. For operations requiring more than one watch, either the commanding officer or a lieutenant-commander should be in command.

Watch Operations.—All operations performed by a watch are supervised by a lieutenant or sub-lieutenant.

A senior officer may be necessary to watch and correct mistakes afterwards on such occasions as a watch drill, but the lieutenant must carry through the work himself.

(*Note.*—If a lieutenant can be given charge of a 20,000 ton ship steaming at 22 knots 2½ cables astern of another equally big ship showing no lights, he can assuredly take entire charge of a watch of seamen, whatever they are told off to do.)

Part of Watch Operations.—Should be delegated by the lieutenant to midshipmen or warrant officers.

For example, after the watch have hoisted a cutter, one part is piped to hoist a whaler and one part to hoist a gig; the lieutenant orders the midshipman of watch to hoist one boat and the warrant officer of the day to hoist the other boat; if hoisted together, the lieutenant gives the orders for hoisting and these junior officers the orders for 'High enough,' 'Ease to life lines,' 'Lie to.'

Provisioning Ship.—If a watch is used, the lieutenant should supervise, not give the orders for hoisting, etc.

A warrant officer or midshipman should be detailed for supervising the derrick work.

Coaling Bills.—The lieutenant of a part of the ship must make out his coaling bills himself to meet all cases (see 'Coaling').

The commander only informs him, for example, that his command consists of 'all fxle men except sailmaker's mate, who is repairing party.'

The lieutenant will also detail the midshipmen and warrant officers allocated to his command for their duties.

Main Derrick.—Junior officers must be supervised at first, but the hoisting in and out of a launch and pinnace should be a lieutenant's work.

The hoisting in and out of picket boats under favourable conditions should also be a lieutenant's work, as soon as they are accustomed to the derrick.

It is a watch operation, and larger weights are constantly moved about elsewhere by men of less intelligence with a very much less efficient body of men under their command.

Small Derricks.—Being a 'part of the watch' operation, should be delegated by the lieutenant to his midshipman or the duty warrant officer.

(Everyone has seen a whaler being hoisted out by seven officers and twenty men.)

Upper Deck and Mess Deck.—It is usual in large ships for a lieutenant-commander to be in charge of the mess deck, and a lieutenant-commander to work under the commander on the upper deck.

The lieutenants of parts of the ship should be in charge of their section of the upper deck and of their mess deck, under the' supervision of these lieutenant-commanders.

If a lieutenant is in command of and responsible in all matters for a division of seamen, he also should be in command of his own mess deck and upper deck.

Supervising the Boats.—The lieutenant on duty should give all orders to the duty boats.

The commander makes out the boat routine and gives the lieutenants his general wishes as to which boats to use for the different trips, but the lieutenant of the watch or day calls away all boats himself, using his discretion and judgment and only referring to the commander when in doubt.

General Drills.—Taking 'In and out nets' as an example, the commander details each lieutenant for a section of the nets, and the lieutenant is entirely responsible that his men are properly stationed and know their duties.

Landing Parties.—Always detail the officers in strict accordance with the strength of the party, i.e. a lieutenant for a company; a midshipman or W.O. for a half company; a commander or lieutenant-commander for full battalion.

It is quite wrong to take the command out of the proper officers' hands as soon as their men are told off for any special work.

Decentralisation: Petty Officers.—*Watch Operations.*—Captains of tops are told by the lieutenants what is required, and themselves detail their men and carry out the orders.

For example, for many watch drills a cutter has to be lowered and a part of the ship are detailed for this. The captain of the top gives the orders for lowering and supervises.

Part of the Watch Operations.—If no warrant officer or midshipman to take command, the senior petty officer is to take command.

Coaling Bills, etc.—The petty officers make out their own bills for such operations as coaling, and submit them to their lieutenants for approval.

General Drills.—Petty officers are told by the lieutenants the number of men required for each operation, and they themselves detail their men.

Parades and Falling in.—The petty officers can be given opportunities of command at all parades. This is fully explained under 'Parades,' p. 68.

Special Parties, etc.—A petty officer's command being a watch of one part of the ship and a leading seaman's a part of a watch of one part of the ship, endeavour should be made to keep to these commands for all special parties, e.g. avoid the not uncommon sight of a petty officer commanding two ordinary seamen with a cart.

CHAPTER VI

DIVISION OF NON-SPECIALIST WORK

The men who form the ship's company are all specialised in some work or other, and each branch has the same amount of work to do.

It is customary for each branch to claim that they are harder worked than any other, but the answer to this is that all work approximately the same number of hours, and certainly all obey the pipe for leave with equal alacrity.

Therefore, all work in connection with the life of the ship that is not specialist work should be undertaken by all branches in proportion to their numbers.

All work in connection with the feeding of the ship's company, all outside working parties, pickets, etc., come under this heading of non-specialist work.

Large Provisioning.—A complete watch of the hands (seamen, stokers, marines) will be required for this.

The lieutenant in charge should be provided with a list of stores to come in and their stowage, and should organise the watch beforehand, detailing the seamen for steamer's hold, receiving, working whips and inhauls, and stowing as far as possible; stokers and marines for stowing. The flour party must be cleaned in white rig.

Daily Provisioning.—A party is required daily for transferring stores from the holds to the issue room and for getting beef to the beef screen.

This party should be taken from the seamen, stoker and marine sweepers in the proper proportion.

The chief boatswain's mate of mess deck, chief stoker, and serjeant of flats are made responsible for telling these men off in rotation.

Working Parties for Non-Specialist Work.—These parties are always to be taken from the three branches in proportion to numbers borne.

The executive officer will find forms like the attached very useful for ordering these parties (1s. per block at any printers).

Examples of work that come under this heading:

Coaling another ship.

Work on recreation grounds.

Loading a lighter with mixed stores.

PARTY FOR NON-SPECIALIST WORK

A party consisting of

Will land for

Time of landing

Time of embarking

Rig

Remarks

Commander
or Commanding Officer.

O.C. marines

Senior engineer-lieutenant

Officer in charge

Officer of the day

Pickets.—Pickets are always told off from the three branches in proportion to numbers borne.

Here, again, an order form like the attached is most useful.

PICKET ORDER		
	P.O.	Others
NUMBERS:—Seamen	..	
Marines	..	
Stokers	..	
Artisans	..	
Time of falling in		
Time of embarking		
Officer required		
	Commander or Commanding Officer.	
Seaman Regulating Office		
Stoker Regulating Office		
Serjeant-major		
Officer of the day		

Hospital Cases.—Cot party should always be formed from the same branch as the sick man.

Cart Parties.—Always formed from the branch who requisitioned the cart—e.g. a seaman cart party should not be sent for stokers' or marines' bags and hammocks.

Storing.—Stores should always be hoisted in and stowed by the branch to which they belong.

This is usually done when drawing from a dockyard, but is not always carried out when a ship or lighter brings a mixed cargo.

If necessary, one or two seamen ratings can be lent for stropping up, etc., but the principle should be carried out as far as possible.

Escorts.—Should always be provided by the branch to which the offender belongs. An escort of seamen can take charge of a seaman offender just as well as an escort of marines; it is a bad look out if they cannot.

Sentry on Cells.—Should be provided by the branch to which the prisoner belongs; badgemen should always be chosen if available.

Note.—The custom of using marines for escorts and cell sentries is not a good one. It cannot be carried out in ships with small marine complements or no marine complement at all, and it would be better to adopt a universal system for the whole service.

The marines, in a proper organisation, have as much work to do as the remainder of the ship's company, and, if used for these duties during a bout of leave-breaking, will be unable to carry out their ship's work properly.

Engine-room Artificers.—Stokers should be told off for hospital parties, cart parties, etc., when requisitioned for E.R.A's; but it is better to employ marines if an escort or a sentry is required for one of this branch.

Coaling Steamboats and Galleys.—This work is on what might be termed the 'halfway line,' but the most efficient arrangement is for the E.R. department to supply parties for this work. The reasons are, firstly, because the E.R. department always has men in a suitable rig for this work; and secondly, because the operation will be under one officer's orders.

Everyone has experienced the case of the steamboat and duty hands being ready but the coal not ready, and also of the reverse situation.

Water Supply.—The custom of telling off a seaman as captain of the hold and letting him look after the water supply dies hard; it should be killed off quickly. The making and controlling of water in a man-of-war is specialist work for the E.R. department, and it is unnecessary for an ancient able seaman to spend his time wandering round the ship checking the work.

CHAPTER VII

STANDING ORDERS

Most executive officers are faced by the difficulty of not knowing when to stop when they are writing out their standing orders. The best rule is 'Stop as soon as you possibly can.'

Long strings of orders are seldom read and often many of them not obeyed, and it is much better to have a few orders which are obeyed implicitly.

The 'N.B.' in the following notice, which was on the walls of a well-known naval establishment for many years, is a humorous example of the misuse of the word 'order.'

Order

No officer is to fill a bath unless he intends to use it immediately.

(Signed)

COMMANDER.

N.B.—This order is to be obeyed (*sic*).

The following eleven orders are given as an example of keeping down the number; they embrace everything necessary, and do not wander into a lot of orders about not spitting on the deck and not throwing vegetables about, which really should not be in print on a modern ship's mess deck.

General Orders.—1. The ordinary customs are to be observed of H.M. service as regards general conduct, smoking, dress, and mess-deck regulation.

2. The use of unseamanlike orders such as 'Hang on,' 'Turn up,' etc., is to be discouraged, and the proper orders, 'Hold on,' 'Belay,' 'Vast hauling,' 'Handsomely,' 'Roundly,' etc., used.

3. Any party of men who have finished the work they have been told off for, are to be fallen in and reported to the commander, commanding officer, or officer of the day.

All parties of men falling in are to fall in 'at ease,' and are to be called to 'attention' by the senior rating present and reported to the commander, commanding officer or officer of the day, and then 'stood at ease' again.

4. No man is ever to leave his work without first obtaining permission from the officer, petty officer, or leading hand, under whose orders he is at the time.

5. The courtesy of standing to one side and showing respect when officers pass is to be given by every man.

6. Card playing is allowed at mess tables and on the upper deck, but any form of gambling is strictly prohibited.

7. Every man who assists at or supervises the closing of a watertight door is to do his work in a thorough manner, as at any time the safety of the ship may depend on the watertightness of a particular door.

8. Any man wishing to see the commander can do so by putting a request in in the service manner.

9. Matches, other than patent safety matches, are not allowed.

10. No man is to go aloft without first asking permission from the officer of the watch and finding out if it is safe to do so from the wireless room.

11. Every man is to be thoroughly acquainted with the attached table, showing men excused certain pipes, so far as it concerns himself.

Notes on these Eleven Orders.—Order No. 1 is possibly unnecessary; it is put in to inform the ship's company that usual customs of the service are in force.

Order No. 2 is placed in these orders so that it is constantly before the men; it is a Herculean task to put this right, but it can be done.

Order No. 3 is a matter of 'fancy waistcoats'; it is admirable all the same.

Order No. 4 dispels 90 per cent, of well-thought-out and well-presented excuses at commanders' defaulters.

Clean Ship.	Divisions	Tricks	Duty Section	Watch for X cise	Watch .	
Scrub decks till 6.40, then under Lieut. (G.)	exc.	exc. 6.0-8.0 am pm	exc. 6.0-8.0 am pm	exc. 6.45-4.0,6.45-4.0 am pm	exc.	Turret Sweepers.
Ditto.	exc.	exc. 6.0-8.0 am pm	exc. 6.0-8.0 am pm	exc. 6.45-4.0 am pm	exc.	Armourer's Party.
Clean ladderways and lobbies.	exc. except Sunday	exc.	exc.	exc.	exc.	Boatswain's Yeo.
Scrub decks till 6.40, then in bath-rooms.	attend	exc. 6.0-6.0 am pm	exc. 6.0-6.0 am pm	attend	exc.	Bathroom Sweepers.
Scrub decks till 6.40, then clean ladderways and lobbies	exc. except Sunday	exc. 6.0-6.0 am pm	exc.	attend	exc.	Sailmaker's Mate.
Clean heads.	A.B. at-tend	exc.	exc.	exc.	exc.	Heads.
Special duties.	exc.	exc.	exc.	exc.	exc.	Hold.
Offwatch, scrub decks.	exc. off watch attend	exc.	exc.	exc.	exc.	Tel. Exchange.
Scrub decks till 6.40, then under Lieut. (G.)	exc.	exc. 6.0-8.0 am pm	exc.	exc. 6.45-4.0 am pm	exc.	G. L.'s Writer.
Clean out their messes.	attend	exc. till 11.15-1.30 am pm 3.30-4.0 pm	exc.	ditto.	exc. till 9.0 am 11.15-1.30 am pm 3.30-4.0 pm	Messmen { P.O. C.P.O. }
Scrub decks till 6.40, then clean.	attend	exc.	exc.	exc. 6.45-8.0,6. am pm	exc.	Messengers.
Under Q.M.	attend	exc.	exc.	exc. 6.45-8.0,6. am pm	exc.	Side Boys (4), Q.M.'s Mess (2).
Under B.M.	attend	exc.	exc.	exc. 6.45-8.0,6. am pm	exc.	Call Boys.
Scrub decks till 6.40, then clean.	attend	exc.	exc.	exc. 6.45-8.0,6. am pm	exc.	Buglers.
Special duties.	exc.	exc.	exc.	exc.	exc.	W.O.'s Servants.
Special duties.	attend	attend	exc. 6.0-6.0 am pm	attend	exc.	Side Party.
Part of ship till after division.	attend	exc. 8.45-6.0 am pm	exc. 8.45-6.0 am pm	attend	exc.	Painting Party.
Special duties.	exc.	exc.	exc.	exc.	exc.	Torpedo Watch-keepers.
Scrub decks till 6.40, then clean.	exc.	exc. 6.0-8.0 am pm	exc.	exc. 6.40-4.0 am pm	exc.	Torpedo Party.
Part of ship till after division.	attend	exc. 6.0-8.0 am pm	exc.	attend	exc.	Boatswain's Party.
Clean boats.	at-tend	..	exc.	at-tend	exc.	Duty Boats.
Scrub decks till 6.40, then clean flats, etc.	attend	attend	exc.	attend	exc.	Sweepers.

Order No. 5 should be most rigidly carried out; a newly commissioned large ship's company will tax the most energetic commander in doing so.

Order No. 7 is included, as it should always be before the men.

Order No. 8 is included, as untrustworthy chief petty or petty officers may prevent a youngster coming forward, and this right must be safeguarded.

Order No. 10 is included, as it should always be before the men.

Order No. 11 dispels the 10 per cent, of excuses left over from Order No. 4.

Excused and Clean Ship Table.—This is printed under the general orders.

Quite respectable-sized volumes have been written on individual duties in a man-of-war, but the type of table on page 60 will cover the whole subject.

CHAPTER VIII

ROUTINE

The daily routine is generally the same in all ships of a squadron, and the following notes are on small variations from these ordered routines.

Sunday Routine.—A peace-time Sunday routine that has met with success is as follows:

6.15. Call the hands. Lash up. Cocoa.
6.45. Hands fall in (includes all stokers not cleaning ship below or on duty).
Clean upper deck and mess deck.
7.10. Gun cleaners to stations.
7.45. Cooks.
7.55. Breakfast.
9.10. Out-pipes.
9.15. Mess cleaners clear up mess deck.
Remainder of seamen fall in, clear up upper deck.
9.45. Divisions.

It will be noticed that the stokers fall in on the upper deck. The object of this is to clear the stokers' mess decks so that their mess cleaners and sweepers can get a chance of doing their work, and also to provide hands to assist in cleaning the upper deck.

They are told off, as described on a previous page, by their parts of the ship to join up with upper deck parts of the ship and assist with the scrubbing or the bright work, preferably the latter. 'Gun cleaners' are two men detailed from each secondary armament gun.

The routine is, of course, dependent on having carried out a proper 'Saturday cleaning' on the day before.

To give all hands a 'steerage hammock' on Sundays is an object to work for if possible.

Cautionary Bugles and Pipes.—It is not sometimes realised how important cautionary bugles and pipes are in modern ships with their numerous bulkheads and large mess decks.

A good plan is to sound a 'G' or pipe a caution five minutes before any actual action is required, during the period known as 'working hours.'

After 'working hours,' a cautionary pipe of ten minutes should be given.

A visit to the mess deck at once shows the necessity for this.

Every commander knows the excuses men give for being adrift from work: 'I was having a wash,' 'I was at my bag and had my clothes off,' 'I was having a shave.'

A percentage of these excuses are generally true, as men do wash, work at their bags, and shave in the dog watches, but they cannot be taken.

Proper cautions avoid all this difficulty.

Forenoon Stand Easy.—A forenoon 'stand easy' as a regular part of the routine is in general use now.

It must, of course, depend on the actual work going on at the time, but there are not many days that this cannot be given.

A great number of petty offences are eradicated, and it affords a definite break during the forenoon, which is used as the finishing time for certain work and the starting time for other work—e.g. hands are told off as follows: 'After stand easy, the first-aid class will muster at the sick bay and the training classes will hoist out the first cutter ready for seamanship instruction in the afternoon.'

Rolling the Drum.—The old custom of rolling the drum round the mess decks at 'out pipes' after a meal hour or 'make and mend' afternoon is a very excellent one.

It rouses sleeping men quicker than any amount of piping by call-boys with squeaky voices.

Routine and Officer of the Watch Board.—A combined duty boat, notice and routine board made out of oak and corticene will last for ever.

The corticene is let into the oak board as shown, and ordinary chalk is used for writing on it.

The board contains the following information:

Name of commanding officer.
Name of officer of the day or watch.
Name of stand-by officer of the day.
Duty watch.
Boat routine.
Duty boats.
Daily routine.
War routine.
Names of duty section.
Keys of leave boards (*q.v.*).
Number of men under punishment.
Special orders.

If times for routine are changed, the new times are written in the column for the purpose—this saves all mistakes.

Rounds.—It is customary to clear the mess deck for 9 o'clock rounds; this perhaps means turning, in a big ship, a thousand men on to the upper deck on a cold, wet night.

That is the intention at least, for in practice many of the thousand play hide-and-seek with the commander, or turn into their hammocks with their clothes on.

A very efficient rounds can be carried out without clearing the mess deck.

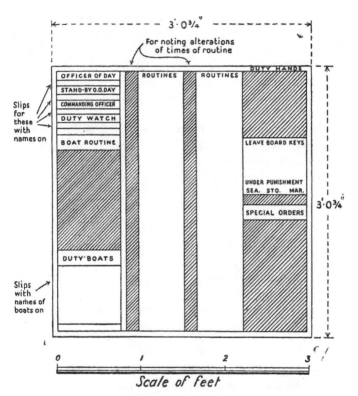

FIG. 1.—ROUTINE AND OFFICER OF WATCH BOARD,
Shaded portion corticene.

The petty officers of mess decks call the men to attention as the rounds pass. If there is fault found, the delinquents are there and hear the commanding officer's remarks.

Clearing up Decks.—On many routines the pipe 'Clear up decks' goes long before it is necessary, and the forenoon and afternoon are thereby considerably curtailed.

For example, before dinner pipe 'Clear up decks' when 'cooks' is sounded. Ten minutes is ample, and the work of the ship is not all stopped twenty or twenty-five minutes before dinner.

Natural Sequence in Routines.—A great deal of time and unnecessary work can be saved if the routine is adjusted so that events which naturally follow one another are kept together.

Here is a comparison between what might be termed a 'good' and a 'bad' routine.

GOOD ROUTINE

3.50. Secure. Cooks.
4.0.   Tea.
4.40. Cooks and sweepers clear up mess deck. Remainder clear up upper deck.
4.50. Night attack stations, or cover and secure guns for night.
5.0.   Evening quarters for inspection.

BAD ROUTINE

3.40. Secure. Clear up decks.
4.0.   Evening quarters for inspection. Tea.
4.40. Cooks and sweepers clear up mess deck. Remainder clear up upper deck.
4.50. Night attack stations, or cover and secure guns for the night.

In the 'bad' routine, in the course of 1 hour 20 minutes the upper deck is cleared up on two occasions and the total time given for it is 30 minutes.

All hands are 'on deck' for night attack stations and also for evening quarters for inspection, therefore these two operations should follow one another directly, not be separated by 50 minutes.

In the 'good' routine, the captains of tops are made responsible that their men clear up whatever mess has been made during the afternoon when the bugle 'Secure' is sounded.

CHAPTER IX

PARADES

I t is not a too drastic criticism to say that the importance of good drill and smartness is often not fully realised.

'What is worth doing at all is worth doing well,' is a very true saying, and if men are fallen in for inspection or for detailing for work, every effort should be made to obtain military precision.

Divisions (see pages 70-1).—As a rule, petty officers and leading seamen take little part in divisions, especially in the case of stoker divisions, when it is usual to see a large body of chief petty and petty officers all fallen in facing their men, but taking no charge.

It is an excellent plan to adopt the system of each watch, in the case of seamen, and each part of the ship, in the case of the stokers, falling in separately under the command of their own petty officers.

The petty officers then give the necessary orders to their men, and follow the inspecting officer (i.e. officer of the division) as he inspects the men.

A very well-ordered parade will result, particularly in the case of stoker divisions, which are usually very large and consequently unhandy for efficient drilling.

The whole of a division moves by order of the officer when closing to or extending from prayers, etc., the petty officers taking charge on the return of their commands to the usual deck positions.

Method of Giving Orders.—It is imperfectly realised by many officers and petty officers that an order given to a body of men is always obeyed in the spirit the order is given.

Only too often one hears the following type of order given as one word 'Frontrank-pastepackmarchstandeasy.'

Men receiving orders like this will never obey smartly, and the executive officer should give strict orders that:

1. Officers and petty officers are always to stand out well clear of their men when giving an order.

2. Orders are always to be given in proper parade manner—i.e. a pause between the cautionary part and the executive part of every order.

One often hears lack of vocal power offered as an excuse for slackness; it really has little or nothing to do with the matter.

An officer with powerful lungs roaring out 'Divisionshun' will never make the men under his command nearly as smart as an officer with a bird-like note giving his order 'Di-vi-sion—(long pause)—'un.'

There is one other excuse which should be trodden on quickly, and that is the excuse that sailors are not soldiers; it were better far never to fall in at all than to allow this argument to be used to palliate the inability of officers or petty officers to get their orders obeyed.

Falling in for Detailing for Work.—Whenever men fall in, they should fall in standing at ease. The chief petty officer, or petty officer who takes the muster, calls the hands to 'attention' before reporting to the officer in charge, and, after reporting present or not present, gives the order to 'stand at ease.'

This seems a small matter, but it is very good for discipline and makes for a smart operation.

Telling off the Hands.—A smart 'telling off' must be the corollary to this falling in.

There is nothing so tedious as a long-drawn-out telling off by a man who does not know what he is going to do before the hands fall in.

FIG. 2.—SHIP'S COMPANY AT DIVISIONS.

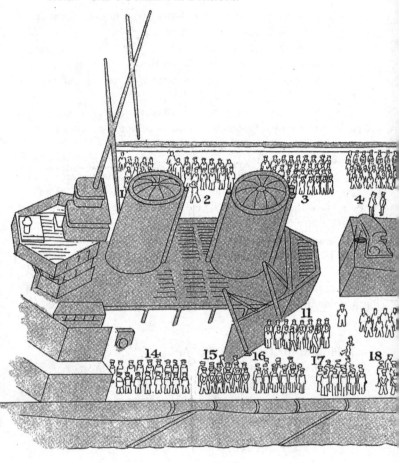

1. Stokers.	A Boiler Room.	7. Stokers.	G Boiler Room.
2. Stokers.	B Boiler Room.	8. Stokers.	Engine Rooms.
3. Stokers.	C Boiler Room	9. Drum and Fife Band.	
4. Stokers.	D Boiler Room.	10. Brass Band.	
5. Stokers.	E Boiler Room.	11. Fxle.	Blue Watch.
6. Stokers.	F Boiler Room.	12. Top.	Blue Watch.

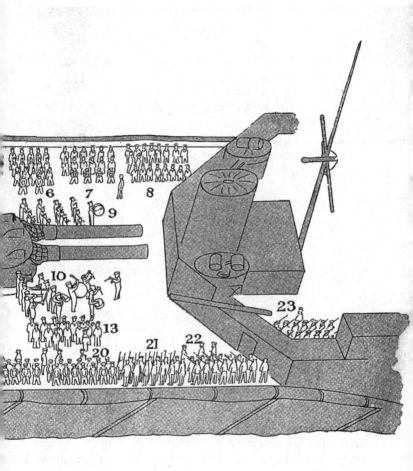

12. Top.   Blue Watch.
13. Q.D.   Blue Watch.
14. Boys.
15. Fxle.   Red Watch.
16. Fxle.   White Watch.
17. Top.   Red Watch.

18. Top.   White Watch.
19. Q.D.   Red Watch.
20. Q.D.   White Watch.
21. Marines.   Red Watch.
22. Marines.   White Watch.
23. Marines.   Blue Watch.

It is an excellent plan to run through the 'telling off' before the time, and, after the hands are reported present, to immediately fall out all the special parties.

After that, the remainder should be quickly told off for work in part of the ship or special work.

Warrant officers' parties should be settled the night before, these officers putting chits in the commander's cabin stating their requirements.

The not uncommon sight of a lot of officers asking for hands, and a kind of 'scrap' going on for the remnants, should be avoided; it is not efficient, and does no good to the men who are being used as the pawns in the game.

Falling in after Work is Completed.—It is customary for men to fall in and be mustered before any work is done, and to fall out indiscriminately when the work is finished. This is only partially true, as sailors, like other people, are not all angels.

An excellent plan, in practice in some ships, is for men to always fall in after the work is finished.

As each party finishes, the P.O. or leading seaman in charge falls them in, calls them to attention, and reports to the officer in charge as, for example, 'Fxlemen Red watch, nets secured for sea.'

When a watch or part of a watch finish their work all together, the senior petty officer present takes the muster and reports to the officer in charge as, for example, 'Red watch, cutter hoisted, falls coiled down.'

This system keeps all the men together until the work in hand is finished, and late on in a commission, when much of the preliminary falling in is dispensed with, is the check on all men being present.

There are also many occasions when there is further work to do with the hands, and it is much better done by completing the first job properly, and then commencing the second job with all hands.

Officers and men not being accustomed to this system, renders it necessary to keep a sharp eye on it for the first week or so. After that it becomes an ordinary part of the ship life.

Dismissing.—Whenever men are dismissed by an officer, they should salute before breaking off.

Orders for the Day.—It is an excellent custom for the commander to read out the programme for the day after morning prayers.

In many ships no one ever knows what is going to happen until they hear a bugle or pipe, and there are many small arrangements that officers and men like to make when they know what is ahead of them.

If some new orders arrive before evening quarters, opportunity can then be taken to make them general knowledge by a pipe.

If new orders arrive before 9 o'clock rounds, the petty officer leading the rounds should announce the purport of the orders as the rounds arrive on each deck.

This is really not a small matter, it is important and makes a great difference in the life of a ship.

Example:—

'Orders for to-day.

Usual routine till noon.

Storeship is expected at 1.0 and will be cleared by the —— watch.

Boys' cutter race against the —— will take place at 4.0.

Cinematograph will be run on the topmen's mess deck at 8.0.

Ship will weigh at 9.30 A.M. tomorrow for subcalibre practice.

Target will be hoisted out when the hands fall in.

Subcalibres will be placed in the guns at cleaning quarters.'

In many ships the information here given is only known to the majority because it is the 'buzz,' whereas it should be known to all hands.

The caution 'D'ye hear there' before a pipe that is intended to disseminate information has, unfortunately, nearly become a thing of the past, but effort should be made to retain it, as in very large ships men pay little attention to pipes if they are not of the watch on board or duty boat's crews.

Duty Hands.—At the beginning of a commission it is a good scheme to prove the duty hands that will take duty from noon of that day when the hands fall in for telling off after divisions. Petty officers and men are not very conversant with their duties in the early days of a commission, and this 'proving' of the duty hands is a certain check on petty officer's forgetfulness and on men being detailed who cannot take duty hand on account of other work.

A slate at the gangway, of course, is an excellent institution, but this double check saves much trouble.

CHAPTER X

COALING

No one would ever venture to lay down the law about coaling organisations, as they must be entirely dependent on the complement and the work which must be done during coaling.

The one maxim which is always true is that every soul who can possibly take part should do so for large coalings.

That this is not always done is apparent. How often one hears a commander of a ship saying to a commander of a sister ship, 'Well, of course you coal quicker, because I never get so many hands as you do.'

This can be greatly obviated if the recommendation in 'Man-of-War Organisation' (Captain Pound, R.N.) is carried out—i.e. that a 'fieldstate' showing the employment of the ship's company is presented to the captain by the commander and engineer-commander.

Stokers for Deck Work.—In a battle cruiser there are usually sufficient stokers available for deck work either to run the barrows or man a hold.

Both have been tried, and the barrow running is the most satisfactory.

The inboard part of coaling then becomes an engine-room department organisation, and the officers, chief petty and petty officers control and know all the men running the coal and tipping it.

For a long coaling, tippers and runners can relieve each other if necessary, which is not possible or desirable if marines or seamen are running the barrows.

The rigging and unrigging of the hold is always a difficulty if the stokers man a hold, and in war or manoeuvre time it is impossible to man the hold with the same men each time, which is a serious handicap.

Coaling Bills.—In peace time the same coaling bill can usually be used for all coalings, and coalings are generally large.

In war or manœuvre time, many different circumstances arise, such as taking in quite small amounts, or arriving in harbour and coaling immediately after high-speed steaming, when no stokers are available.

The following coaling bills have been found necessary in a battle cruiser:

Full Peace Coaling Bill.—Holds.—Seamen and marines.

Barrows, tipping, trimming.—Stokers.

Dumps, artisans, C.P.O.'s and P.O.'s, not captains of tops, and eight stokers per dump.

Full War Coaling Bill.—Same as above, but seamen and marines to strengthen dumps in place of stokers. Men specially required for work on armament excused.

Emergency Coaling Bill (immediate coaling after high-speed steaming and steam up).—Seamen and marines in this case take the barrows and strengthen the dumps. Men specially required for work on armament excused.

Medium Coaling Bill (300 to 400 tons).—Stokers as for full peace coaling bill, except no stokers for dumps.

Seamen and marines for the dumps.

Pantry men, certain marine servants, and artisans carry on with their work.

Small Coaling Bill (under 300 tons).—Seamen and marines for dumps and barrows.

If very small, band plays.

Pantry men, certain marine servants, and artisans carry on with their own work.

One officer per hold only required.

Note.—It is to be remembered that it is *no use employing every available man* for small coalings, as the coal cannot be stowed, and a steady input a little ahead of the speed of stowage is the requirement. Finish up, certainly, with a large number of bags stacked; but, stopping in the middle because there are no more empty bags, is bad management.

Organisation on the Block System.—By this is meant that the complete organisation of each hold is made out by the senior officer of the hold.

He is responsible for detailing, from his coaling bills, bag returners, bag distributors, and filling gangs for all coalings, and barrow men and dumping parties when using the full war, emergency, medium, or small coaling bills.

This in practice works well, as if, for example, he is called on to provide barrow men for his hold, he tells off two complete gangs.

Falling in before Coaling not Necessary.—After the first coaling, falling in is not necessary, and if done in the dark is a waste of time.

A long and tedious muster is much better replaced by the hold gangers, petty officers of barrow parties, and leading hands of bag returners reporting to the officer of their 'block' that their men are present or not present.

A quite undistinguishable mass of men with petty officers going through the 'motions' of mustering them every time it is required to start coaling, is a sight to be seen in some ships, but not to be reproduced if time-saving is the object in view.

Outhaul.—A serviceable fitting, which saves manual labour, is made by shackling a 1-inch wire pendant to the collier's whip and reeving it through a thimble secured to the rigging, or any suitable fitting on the outboard side of the collier, and loading it with a round shot.

Pendant for Whip.—If the collier's derricks are long and give plenty of 'hoist,' an excellent fitting is a 3-foot wire pendant, carrying the hook, shackled to the junction of the whip and inhaul—the hook is easier handled in the collier and the inhaul never takes foul turns round the hook or gets under the bags.

Auxiliary Guys.—The handiest auxiliary guys are single wire pendants fitted with an eye one end to shackle to own part.

Rope Ladders.—Ladders for the men to get in and out of the hold quickly are essential, and should be part of gear taken to the collier when rigging.

Stowing Coaling Gear.—Nets for catching bags, outhauls, spare whips, strops, rope ladders, auxiliary guys, should all be kept *together* by the captains of tops in a proper stowage.

Officers' Meals during Coaling.—If the flats or passages outside officers' messes are large enough, close these messes during coaling and use trestle tables outside the messes for all meals. It is a great luxury to be able to use a clean mess as soon as one is clean oneself.

Plates for Scuppers.—The scuppers must be closed during coaling, and it is a good plan to make proper scupper plates instead of nailing boards over every time the ship is coaled. The boards sometimes get knocked off, and then there is no end of trouble. In some ships, where the drains from turrets lead in to the scupper pipes, it is possible to find an unpleasant mixture of coal and water in the turret, if the bottom of the scupper pipe is choked by coal and the turret drain on a lower level than the upper deck scupper.

These plates are placed in the charge of the plumber, whose duty it is to put them on before coaling and take them off after the deck is swept.

Brooms for Dumping Grounds.—The carpenter should make wooden brooms for each dump before the first coaling. Captains of tops, if worth their salt, will have locked up all the ordinary brooms, and dumping grounds soon get bad for the wheels of the barrows if not swept clear.

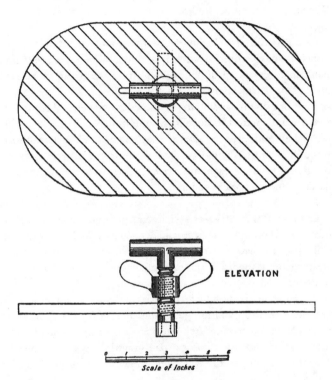

FIG. 3.—COVER FOR SCUPPERS WHILST COALING.

Hazel Rod Fenders.—Select a stowage that is plumbed by a derrick, and make a many-legged sling to take several at a time.

When placing these fenders, hoist them out and float them to their proper positions; do the same for returning them, and so wash all the coal dust out before hoisting in.

Coaling Suits.—Coaling suits are a source of trouble if not properly looked after. The custom of scrubbing them and hanging them up to dry is no doubt a good one when it can be carried out, but only too often this scheme falls through, owing to bad weather or ship proceeding to sea immediately after coaling; in war or manœuvre periods it is well-nigh impossible.

A scheme adopted in some of H.M. ships, which is successful, is to supply each mess with a painted bag. A proper stowage is found for these bags near each mess, and coaling suits are shaken and placed in the bags after coaling.

Endless Band Stowers.—The endless band system, which is greatly in use on shore, is not generally known or used in H.M. ships.

There are many ways in which this system can be advantageously used, and the example chosen is a coal bag stower in one of H.M. ships.

In this case six hundred coal bags are stowed underneath a searchlight platform, and, using the ordinary hand-to-hand throwing, the operation of stowing took ten men about three-quarters of an hour; with the 'stower' the bags were stowed in twelve minutes by four men, thereby greatly facilitating the cleaning of the ship after coaling.

The canvas band is kept running round at fair speed, and the bags are thrown on to the band; the band will throw the bags well clear at the top if the motor is run fast enough.

Derricks for Coaling.—Stow all coaling derricks in their proper position or as near to it as possible, and keep the guys and topping lifts always on the derricks.

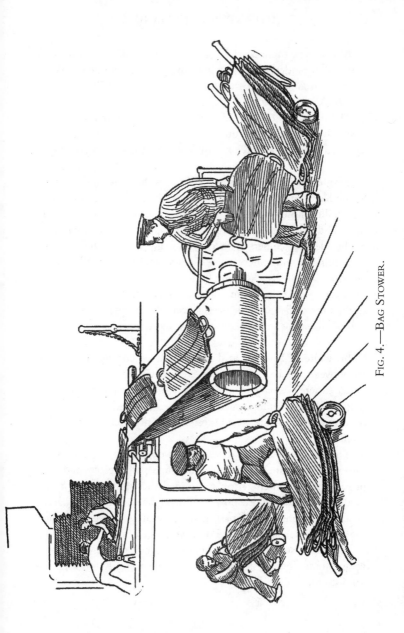

Fig. 4.—Bag Stower.

Always have these derricks ready for all coalings; it is too late to start rigging a derrick and unearthing guys and topping lifts and whips from some out-of-the-way stowage *after* the collier's winches have broken down.

There is a prevalent idea that guys and topping lifts are unsightly and should be out of sight; this is not so if the gear is tautened along the derrick and kept in place by canvas bands.

Single Derrick Coaling.—With the long derricks supplied to modern ships and efficient bollards, coaling from a single derrick collier should be nearly as fast an operation as coaling from a double derrick collier. This does not apply to one or two of the double derrick colliers with exceptionally fast winches, but is a good thing to remember if there are doubts about the collier fitting properly or the derricks being quite long enough.

A very good rule is 'If in doubt, use single derrick system'; to try and use the collier's double derricks, simply because she is so fitted, will often lead to much waste of time and temper.

Stowage of Shovels and Bags.—When coalings are few and far between, the bags and shovels are suitably stowed in the locker because there is usually plenty of time to get them up and distribute them at the dumping grounds; but when coalings are of frequent occurrence and at unexpected times, it is a great advantage to stow them on the upper deck.

The argument against stowing bags on the upper deck is that they may catch fire, but if stowed in four separate places and hoses played on them when 'action' is sounded, there is not much danger of this; whereas a thousand bags impregnated with newly hewn coal stowed tight in a compartment may well cause a furnace, and if the compartment was flooded they would be of no use for coaling.

If bags are stowed on the upper deck, they should be stropped up in bundles before stowing, so that they are ready for whipping out into the collier.

In any case when bags are being collected on the dumps ready for coaling they should be stropped up; the bags can then be swung out and placed in the centre of the hold ready for distributing.

Shovels, if stowed on upper deck, should be rove on iron or wooden bars; each part of the ship having its own bar.

CHAPTER XI

CABLE WORK

Mooring Ship.—The use of the mooring pendant and joggle shackle has been to a great extent discontinued in modern heavy-cabled ships.

A method now in common use, which brings little strain and ensures neither cable being, at any time during the mooring, held by any means except the properly tested Blake slip stopper, is as follows:

Gear Required.—A wire for hauling round an inboard end.

Mooring Six on Each.—Heave in first cable and veer second cable to sixth shackles just abaft Blake slip stoppers.

On stoppers and break cables at sixth shackles.

Insert mooring swivel into one cable, and haul round the inboard end of the other cable by the small wire and shackle it to the swivel.

Heave in to take off the stopper, and then, by veering one cable holder and heaving the other, transfer the swivel to the opposite hawse pipe.

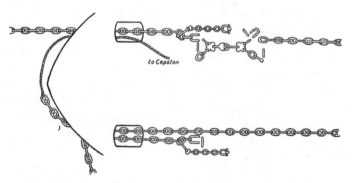

FIG. 5.—PUTTING SWIVEL IN STARBOARD CABLE; HAULING ROUND PORT INBOARD END.

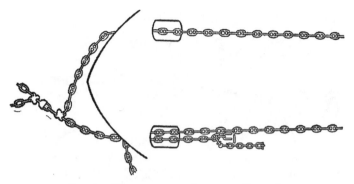

FIG. 6.—TRANSFERRING SWIVEL TO PORT SIDE.

When transferred, shackle on the other outboard end, then heave to take the stopper off and veer the swivel to the required position.

Whichever cable the ship is riding by will be found the best cable to put the swivel in before transferring, as then the transferring can be done with little or no strain, the swivel passing out of the first hawse pipe and into the second hawse pipe in straight lines. If the ship lies as for 'open hawse,' it is immaterial, and some strain must be incurred in dragging the swivel round the bows.

Note.—When transferring, a party is required to haul forward slack cable when the strain is taken by the opposite cable to that in which the swivel was first placed, as there is nothing to draw the cable out, and it will jamb on the cable holder if not hauled off.

Securing to a Buoy.—Heavy-cabled ships seldom secure to a buoy, so the following procedure, which was in use in a flagship that frequently secured to a buoy, may be usefully recorded.

Preparation.—Catting pendant rove and shackled to anchor.

Two and a half-inch hauling forward wire rove through block right forward.

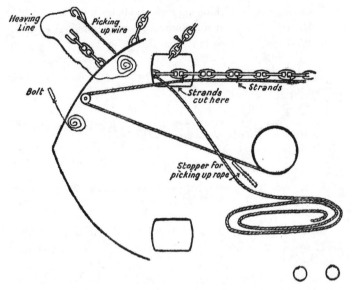

FIG. 7.—SECURING TO A BUOY.

Stopper suitably placed for stoppering picking-up rope.

Small eye-bolt screwed into bolt of anchor shackle.

Procedure.—1. Connect capstan and cable holder and cat the anchor. Lash the end of the lengthening piece to a bolt at the hawse pipe (see Note 1).

2. Place an anchor shackle through the end link the reverse way (see Note 2).

3. Haul forward and pay down the cable through the hawse pipe by the hauling forward wire (see Note 3).

4. On brake, disconnect cable holder.

5. Pay down picking-up rope ready for boat to take; heaving line coiled down on fxle (see Note 4).

6. When picking-up rope is secured to buoy, bring it to capstan and heave buoy close up.

7. On stopper on picking-up rope and belay it (see Note 5).

8. Disconnect capstan and connect up cable holder.

9. Work cable holder so that shackle can be slipped over ring of buoy and bolt passed.

10. Take strain off picking-up rope by heaving in cable and take picking-up rope off.

Note 1.—These bolts at hawse pipe are not usually fitted to a ship building, but they are extremely useful for many purposes.

Note 2.—The usual method is to lower the shackle by a line to the buoy, and for the men on the buoy to reeve it up through the ring and then haul the end link over for shackling on.

This is very difficult work with heavy cables, and the shackle *will pass through the end link the reverse way,* and there is no apparent reason why the bolt should not take the 'pull' of the buoy ring instead of the bow of the shackle.

Note 3.—A number of men with strands should seize every fourth link or so to the hauling forward wire, so that the whole cable travels along the deck.

Note 4.—The boat when lowered is hauled forward by the grass line; she slips this line when hauled well forward and pulls straight to the buoy. A hauling line is made fast to the buoy, and the boat then pulls back to the ship, boats the oars and takes the picking-up rope heaving line. The boat's crew haul in the end of the picking-up rope, and then, facing forward, haul their boat and wire back to the buoy and secure the wire.

The benefit of employing this method is not very apparent in calm, still water, but with a strong tide running and a choppy sea, it is the only sure method of sending the cutter and wire to the buoy.

Note 5.—This stoppering of the picking-up rope in order to belay it, is only done to release hands for other work.

Weighing by Hand. On the Fxle of a Modern Heavy-cabled Ship.

Note.—The sheet cable holder is not sufficiently 'alive' to admit of the cable passing round it before passing through the navel pipe.

This is a quick method of bringing to the cable:

1. On Blake slip stopper.

2. By means of hauling forward wire (which is led through a block right forward in the bows) haul up enough slack cable to throw the cable off the holder.

3. Unhook the wire, turn over the block in the bows, and reverse the lead so that the wire leads back from the bow block outside the rollers on opposite side to sheet cable.

4. Haul up cable by fleets with this wire until there is enough cable to throw over capstan rollers.

Working the compressor is the most satisfactory method of holding the cable whilst throwing off the holder and whilst fleeting the hook.

Two long hook ropes should be used by the men hauling the cable off the capstan as the anchor is being weighed; as each hook rope is hauled home, it is dropped, and the other hook rope, which has been hooked to a new link in the meanwhile, is manned and hauled home.

Pendant for Laying Out Bower or Sheet

Anchor.—Measure this so that when shackled on to the sheet anchor it is just not long enough to reach the sheet dummy cable holder; then, to lower the anchor to the boat, shackle the mooring pendant to this anchor pendant and lower with the capstan, using the dummy sheet cable holder as a fairleader.

Cable Jack.—Cable jacks are in general use now, though not a service fitting. They are indispensable for working modern heavy cables. Putting on slips and shackling or unshackling the mooring swivel is simple work with the heaviest cables if a jack is used. A small 'jack party' work it on the forecastle.

Foul Hawse.—Practically the only case of foul hawse that occurs in a modern ship is one anchor picking up the cable of the other anchor. Hanging the foul cable by joggle shackle and mooring pendant usually clears this foul. If a second hanger is required, a wire hawser shackled to the clear hawse slip forms the other hanger. It is astonishing how few people know that the axis pin of the roller in a clear hawse slip takes the eye of a wire hawser.

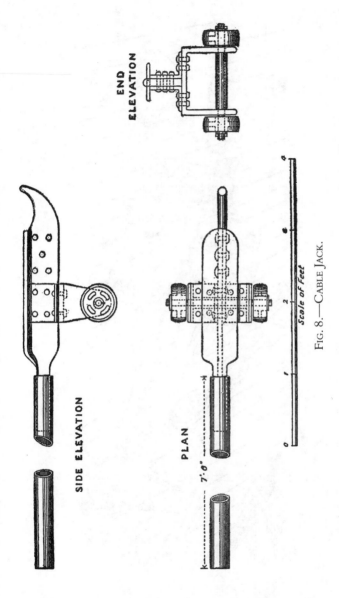

END ELEVATION

SIDE ELEVATION

PLAN

7' 0"

Scale of Feet

FIG. 8.—CABLE JACK.

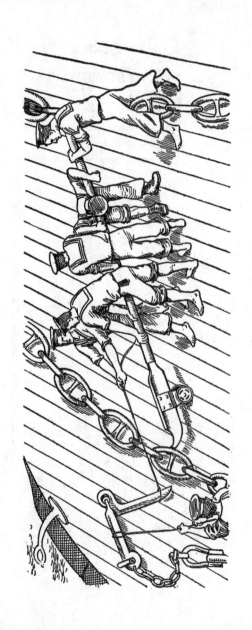

CHAPTER XII

BOATS AND BOAT WORK

Picket **Boat Slings.**—These are supplied with two long legs and a short leg for centre chain.

A more serviceable fitting is to cut the two long legs in two pendants, and fit rings to the picket boat pendants and hooks to the sling pendants.

When lowered to the water, the boat's crew simply unhook the three hooks, and the slings are taken back inboard; but the real benefit is when hooking on for hoisting, and this is made a relatively easy work for the boat's crew, whatever the state of the weather.

Picket Boat Oil Lights.—These are often kept in the lamp room till required. Sooner or later this leads to trouble, when the boat is away from the ship and is delayed returning till after dark.

A rack for bow and steaming lights should be fitted in the fxle of picket boats, and a stowage for a small can of oil.

The crew should be able to trim and keep in order their own lights. The crews of small craft all the world over do it.

Picket Boat Illuminated Sign.—This is a useful fitting that several ships have adopted to show to which ship the boat belongs when at a landing-place or going alongside a ship at night.

It should be made to pivot so that it can be turned towards the steps or ship, as the case may be.

Picket Boat Collision Mat.—A very small collision mat is a useful addition to a picket boat's gear.

Weed trap choked five miles from anywhere is a situation that has been saved by one of these small mats.

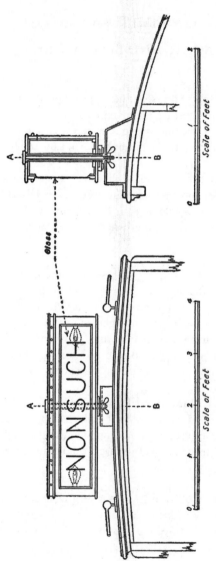

Fig. 9.—Illuminated Box for Ship's Name on Picket Boats.

Picket Boat Spare-wheel Ropes.—Make and keep in each boat a set of spare-wheel ropes. It is very disconcerting to carry away a wheel rope when half-way off to a ship on a nasty night.

Picket Boat Towing Span.—In general use is a towing arrangement, consisting of a hook and two wire pendants taken to the quarter bollards, kept permanently fitted.

FIG. 10.—PICKET BOAT TOWING SPAN.

Painters of boats must be reversed and the thimble placed over the hook for towing, the other end being eased and turned up round the wooden towing bollard.

Coaling Steamboats.—On arrival in harbour always find out if there is a coal hulk or heap from which steamboats can coal.

A great deal of trouble and dirt can be saved if steamboats can fill their bunkers away from the ship.

Small Boat Derricks.—Small boat derricks are usually fitted to stow horizontal, and the purchase for the topping lift is then fitted to work along the deck.

This purchase, which is fairly cumbersome, must in that case be made up and stowed away when the derrick is not in use, in order to keep the gangway clear. This means delay in preparing the derrick for work, and is also a nuisance if the derrick is kept topped for any purpose.

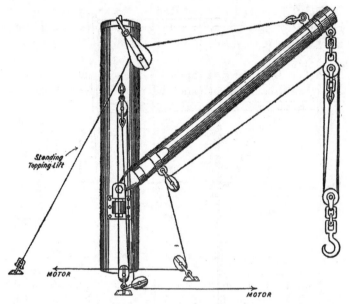

FIG. 11.—SMALL BOAT DERRICK.

These disadvantages disappear if the topping lift is shortened and the purchase fitted to work up and down the mast.

The derrick, of course, cannot be drooped so far, as the upper block has not sufficient travel, but there is ample scope for all derrick work.

This method of fitting necessitates a standing topping lift, and the simplest form is a pendant tailed into the end of the topping lift, which shackles, when the derrick is at forty-five degrees, to a bolt in the deck.

Rack for Oars, Spars, etc.—In many ships the smaller boats stow inside one another, and the boat's gear is kept outside the boats.

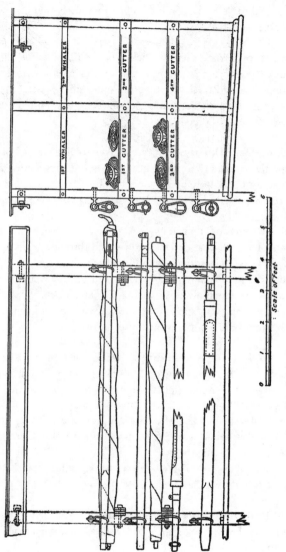

FIG. 12.—STOWAGE FOR BOAT'S MASTS, SAILS, ETC.

A rack with bays, as shown in sketch, is extremely useful. Each boat has a bay as shown.

Stowage of Extra Gear.—Picket boat's masts to be slung along picket boat's crutches on outer side. Bower anchor wire slings to be stopped along launch's crutches on outer side.

These slings are passed round launch before she is hoisted out if 'Out bower anchor' is piped.

Working Derrick Guys.—If care is taken to pipe which boat is going out, the captains of tops practically work the guys themselves.

It is extraordinary how often one sees a boat going out, and no one on the guys having the least idea what is actually happening.

Heel Fittings of Derricks.—A sudden discovery that the 'tulip end' of a small boat derrick had twisted through nearly sixty degrees shows the necessity of examining these fittings.

If the goose neck is not working freely, and a heavy weight, such as a cutter, is guyed rapidly, this twisting may take place.

There is nothing very apparent to the eye when it has happened; hence the importance of occasional inspection.

Boat-hooks for Sounding.—Mark all picket boat's boat-hooks in feet, so that correct soundings can be called when creeping slowly to a landing-place where depth is not known.

Tide Table.—Always have at the gangway a tide table when anchored in harbours where the boat landing-places are not accessible at certain states of tide.

Coxswains of picket boats to always look at this table before leaving the ship for the shore.

Oars for Lifeboat.—Fourteen-foot oars (thirteen-foot for bowmen) are the best oars in a bad sea, when longer oars are difficult to control.

Hoisting Cutter.—If motor bollards are available, train the cutters' crews to hoist their own boats. This does not mean that the boats should be hoisted by this means as a practice; the evolution of running the boats up by hand should always be done when hands are available.

But it is a great comfort under certain circumstances to be able to pipe 'Away first cutters, hoist your boat.'

Ordering Power on the Derrick.—Supply the officer of the watches with a proper chit for ordering power of this type:

Main Derrick

Power is required on main derrick $\begin{array}{l}\text{Purchase}\\ \text{topping}\end{array}$

lift at . . . .

    for (*a*) Light boats only.
        (*b*) Picket boats.
        (*c*) Light boats emergency.
        (*d*) Picket boats emergency.
        (Cross out the three not required.)

This chit is sent to the duty derrick petty officer, and it is his duty to inform all concerned and report the derrick ready at the time ordered.

Purchase and topping lift are both shown on the chit, as at times power is only required for lowering a boat which has been 'hung' temporarily on the derrick, and the power required is little.

A good illustration of the necessity of an order form of this kind is only found when power is ordered immediately after exercising breakdowns at general quarters. If a messenger then runs straight to the switchboard room and orders power, the watchkeeper there may do some serious damage by making switches.

(*c*) and (*d*) refer to electric hoists, and are to be reserved for real cases of emergency, such as a badly damaged boat requiring immediate hoisting. The P.O. then knows that every other circuit in the ship must be broken if necessary to supply the power.

The distinction is drawn between light and heavy boats, as much more power is required for a picket boat than for a launch or pinnace, the former probably necessitating a third dynamo being started.

Boat Ropes and Stern Fasts.—An efficient boat rope is made by reeving the rope through a 15-inch lignum-vitæ bull's-eye hung from the boom by a 2-inch wire pendant.

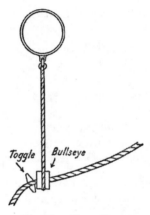

FIG. 13.—BOAT ROPE.

The rope must have a toggle fitted to prevent it unreeving.

These bull's-eyes are difficult to obtain. They do exist in H.M. dockyards.

These boat ropes remain on permanently in harbour.

Boat ropes and stern fasts should be kept on special reels as near their boom as possible when not in use.

If the ship has quarter booms, lead the stern fast through a block on the quarter boom; the boats lie clearer than if taken from the ship's side.

Hoisting Launch and Pinnace at Catting Roller.—Many modern ships have sufficient flare of the bows to admit of the launch and pinnace being hoisted at the catting roller.

If this is possible, it is well worth while making pendants for this purpose, as many circumstances arise when it is extremely useful to be able to hoist boats forward as a temporary measure.

For launch, the pendant should be long enough to be taken to the capstan.

For pinnace, a brailing purchase is used shackled to the pendant, and the fall is taken to a motor bollard.

Picket Boat Rubbers.—The carpenter must prepare spare lengths of rubber as soon as possible, so that repair of rubber, which has to be frequently undertaken, can be done in quick time.

Make these spare rubbers of a slightly larger size than those usually fitted to picket boats—it pays.

Also, if not thought too unbecoming, ekings on the upper stem are very useful when ship lies at badly sheltered anchorages where picket boats have to make fast astern.

Life Lines for Small Boats.—Whaler's, gig's, and galley's davits are often not fitted with life lines—instead, when the boat is up, a few hands hold on before all, and somebody calls out that delightful expression, 'Come up behind.' Fit life lines, or it is certain that sooner or later there will be an accident—a whaler half full of water is not an easy boat for two or three men to hold on to.

Transporting Trolley.—Two transporting trolleys, similar to those in use in a boat shed, are a valuable asset in a ship.

Boats, ladders, wash-deck lockers, etc., can all be moved about with the greatest ease.

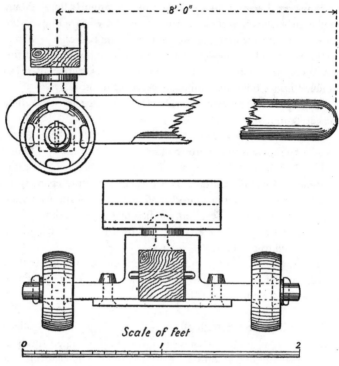

FIG. 14 .—BOAT TRANSPORTING TROLLEY.

TRANSPORING A LADDER.

Starting Boat Races.—An excellent system adopted for a regatta in 1914 was as follows.

The principal starter took up a position by one of the starting buoys and used flags to indicate which way boats were required to move. The flags used were the racing flags of the different ships, but numeral flags would have done equally well.

Flag held towards the finishing line signified 'pull up'; flag held vertical signified 'hold water'; flag held towards the starting line signified 'back water.'

One or more assistant starters, from steamboats in rear of the line of boats, adjusted the line by watching the flags and ordering the boats accordingly. There was very little delay on the starting line as a result of using this system, and extremely accurate starts.

CHAPTER XIII

CLEANING SHIP AND ODDS AND ENDS

The subject of cleaning ship has naturally been almost exhausted in the various books written for the benefit of executive officers, and the items here are a few useful 'tips' that have been collected and are not universal knowledge.

Holystones.—The decks of modern ships are too spacious, as a rule, to holystone all over in the time available, if the service holystones are used by men working on the knee, and ships are consequently reduced to holystoning sections of the deck at a time.

The whole deck can be thoroughly holystoned if the merchant ship type of handle and holder is used.

This holder will either take the merchant ship large holystone or four service holystones; it is not worth the expense to buy the large holystones.

The seamen must use the full scope of the handle, and great power can be brought on to the holystone by keeping pressure on the middle of the handle.

Small holystones with a hole in the middle, used with a broom handle, do the corners as usual.

Cleaning Down Screens.—Proper hooked spars with brackets for planks are well worth making for cleaning down or painting high screens.

A deal of time is saved, and a lot of untidy paraphernalia, if each part of the ship is supplied with these spars.

Ladder Stanchions.—These, only too often, are thrown into a locker on proceeding to sea and brought out green on arrival in

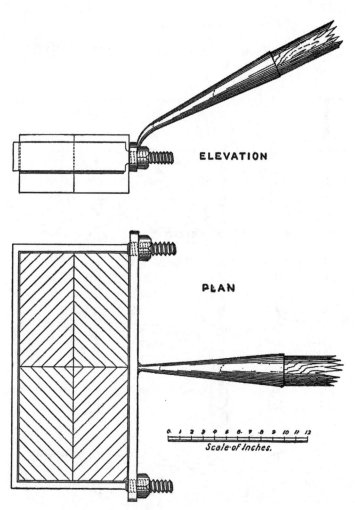

ELEVATION

PLAN

0 1 2 3 4 5 6 7 8 9 10 11 12
Scale of Inches.

FIG. 15.—HOLDER FOR HOLYSTONES.

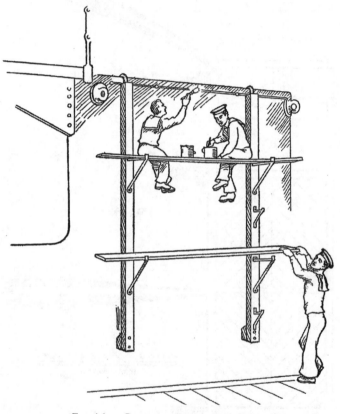

Fig. 16.—Cleaning Down Screens.

harbour, necessitating a hurried cleaning to be in time for the first important person going over the side.

This can be obviated by making a proper rack in the nearest lobby to the ladder; not only are they always clean, but are considerable ornament to the lobby.

Stove Funnels.—The service stove funnel is ugly and requires stays.

Very handsome and easily cleaned funnels can be made out of copper exhaust piping. The length of piping is screwed to the deck fitting and splayed out at the top and fitted with a cap.

This piping can be picked up in many shipyards.

Hatch Clips.—The butterfly nuts are so numerous in many ships that it is out of the question to attempt to polish them.

Nothing is so unpleasant to the eye as dirty brass, and these butterflies can be made respectable by painting with Japan black.

Scuppers.—Scuppers are often badly placed for running the water off the upper deck, and a number of men have to be employed drying up round stanchions and deck fittings.

This can all be saved by running an inner cant along inside the deck fittings and cementing between the two cants.

The cement is kept whitewashed, and the whole deck is much cleaner and easier to dry up.

Staining Bread Barges.—Brass hoops on bread barges are difficult to clean if the wood is kept white; also the bread has to be returned to a damp barge after scrubbing.

A very smart and efficient method of treating bread barges is to stain them with diluted Condy's fluid.

This gives them the appearance of old oak, and can be varnished if desired to further improve their appearance.

Paint Pots.—By far the best paint pots are those made from the service malt tin; these pots are light and hold plenty of paint, and should be collected from the day of commissioning.

Preparing for Painting.—Always place all stages, spars, etc., along the net shelf the night before the side is to be painted. An immediate start in the morning makes all the difference.

Dustpans.—The service dustpan invariably disappears after very short service. Good solid brass dustpans well repay the trouble of making; they will last the whole commission, and are not only useful but ornamental.

Tallies.—It is not universally known that tallies and bunker louvre plates can be made easy to clean and ornamental by running hot sealing-wax into them and then rubbing down till the letters appear.

Boot Racks.—Boot racks in the ship's side are usually untidy, and, being out of sight, lead to dirt.

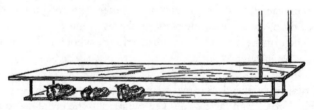

Fig. 17.—Mess Table fitted with Boot Shelf.

Plain racks for the boots under the tables are easily made by the artisans, and are much preferable.

Hose Fittings.—The neatest way to stow the hose fittings is to screw the branch pipes on to the caps, which are hung by small chains.

Only a plain bracket is then required for the hose, which is made up on the bight, and several unnecessary fittings are thus done away with.

Painting where Traffic Heavy.—At canteen and round the galley, imitation brickwork varnished over will keep well for at least six months and probably longer.

Additional Sleeping Billets.—Hammock hooks should be fitted in as many covered-in portions of the upper deck as possible—e.g. partially covered or wholly covered secondary armament batteries.

A large number of men will request to sleep in the open air in summer; and if this is made possible, the sick list will soon show the effect.

Clocks.—Canteen committee should purchase clocks for all mess decks as soon as possible.

Clocks and cautionary pipes (mentioned under 'routine') have a remarkable effect on the rapidity of falling in, and cannot, in the very large ships of the present day, be regarded merely as a luxury.

Drying Room.—As a general rule the drying room will not take nearly all the clothes required.

If there is a suitable stokehold casing, it is a good plan to fit proper wire clotheslines in it as an additional drying room.

Secret drying places will be much reduced, if not removed altogether. Encourage washing, even at the cost of breaking some hitherto fixed ideas on the sacredness of certain compartments.

Heads.—Most captains of the heads have a habit of closing up the whole of the heads for a considerable time before inspections.

With a very large ship's company this is undesirable, and can be avoided by fitting iron bars to bar off a certain part of the heads. The captain of the heads has permission to put these bars up at a certain time before inspections and for daily cleaning.

The discomfort caused by a long closing of the heads is usually only brought to the executive officer's notice by the medical officer.

Whether or not smoking should be permitted in the heads in non-working hours is a matter of controversy.

No bad results are apparent in the ships where it is permitted, but it is of course confined to non-working hours.

If allowed, orders *re* not smoking in the heads in service hours and loitering must be rigidly obeyed.

Guard Rails.—Steel or brass elbow high guard rails, run right round the smooth paintwork surfaces of the mess deck, will repay the trouble of fitting a thousandfold.

The blacksmith can easily run them up, provided he can get the material.

Waste-paper Barges.—Brass-bound paper barges on the mess decks are of great assistance in keeping the decks tidy.

Unless something is provided, paper and kindred rubbish is thrown on the deck and remains there till the sweeper clears up.

Chest Covers.—It being a golden rule never to cover up a dirty place or object by a clean cover, it is not very apparent why chest covers are still in use.

Chests painted with white and black enamel, and the name-plates well polished, always look well. Chest covers rarely look respectable, as they soon assume different appearances from age or the idiosyncrasies of washerwomen.

The tops can be frequently painted if a rapid drying mixture is kept for the purpose.

Such a mixture can be made as follows:

Gum shellac.

Methylated spirits.

Vegetable black.

Paying Money.—With a large ship's company it is a good plan to pay at two separate tables at the same time. The rough ledger is kept in two parts—namely, engine-room ratings and remainder.

Nets for Stores and Provisions.—These are not supplied, and should be made as soon as possible if anything like rapid work is aimed at.

Two are required, one being filled whilst the other is being hoisted in and cleared.

A good type is a 12-foot square wire net, made with 1-inch wire and with a 6-inch mesh; large eyes are worked in the corners for the hook.

These nets can be loaded up quickly with a large number of cases or casks or flour bags.

Targets.—The best target that has been designed lately for dropping, and one that will stand considerable sea and wind, is of a pyramid shape as shown in the sketch (overleaf).

Whatever target is used, always use some old rope for steadying lines, and let them go when the target is dropped. It is a distressing sight to see a target dropped and capsized by a steadying line that has jambed and that has not been able to be slipped because it is the end of a fall.

For all small target towing work it is a good plan to lead the tow rope through a block at the derrick head.

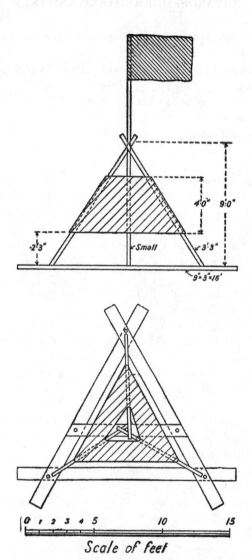

4'0"

9'0"

2'3"

Small

3'3"

9"×3"×16'

0 1 2 3 4 5   10   15

Scale of feet

FIG. 18.—TRIANGULAR TARGET.

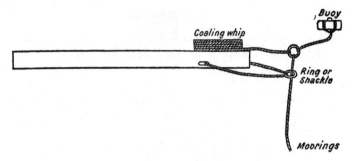

FIG. 19.—TARGET MOORINGS.

The target is slipped as usual by strop and toggle, and the tow rope paid out through the block; then, when the practice is finished, heaving in on the tow rope will bring the target up bows first to the derrick head, when the purchase can be hooked on at leisure.

An excellent method of laying out a target that has to be picked up after firing is shown in the sketch (above).

However bad the weather, if the ship can get hold of the coaling whip, the moorings can be weighed and the target dropped under the derrick afterwards.

Cooking Dinners.—A good plan is to divide the messes up into several equal sections and post up a programme. The ship's steward, when issuing the meat, issues those portions which are suitable for the form of cooking on the programme, which is a great advantage.

Also a mess, knowing that, for example, they are to have a pot mess next day, can order carrots, onions, tinned tomatoes, seasoning, etc., from the canteen the night before.

Butcher.—The refrigerator is often a considerable distance from the beef screen, and the work of transferring beef is greatly simplified by fitting a small derrick at the nearest uptake to the upper deck.

PROGRAMME.

Messes	Monday	Tuesday	Wednesday	Thursday	Friday	Saturday	Sunday
1–12	Steam Pie	Hash	Roast	Pot	Baked Pie	Roast	Steak
13–26	Steak	Steam Pie	Hash	Roast	Pot	Baked Pie	Roast
27–37	Roast	Steak	Steam Pie	Hash	Roast	Pot	Baked Pie
38–50	Baked Pie	Roast	Steak	Steam Pie	Hash	Roast	Pot
52–60	Pot	Baked Pie	Roast	Steak	Steam Pie	Hash	Roast
61–75	Roast	Pot	Baked Pie	Roast	Steak	Steam Pie	Hash
75–82	Hash	Roast	Pot	Baked Pie	Roast	Steak	Steam Pie

In many ships this will be a 'light and vent' shaft.

If there is a motor bollard near, this daily work of transferring then requires about 10 per cent, of the usual number of hands.

Issue of Slops.—Issue every day, except Sunday and Tuesday, between 12.30 and 1.0, and the ordinary routine of the ship is never interfered with.

Tuesday is the day for issuing sugar, tea, etc.

Additional Canteen.—In many large complement ships there is only one serving window at the canteen, and it is not an uncommon thing for men to go without supper owing to the large numbers being served.

A great number only go to buy cigarettes, writing-paper, etc., and an excellent plan is to build or utilise a suitable place for a dry-goods canteen.

This canteen opens and closes at the same hours as the main canteen, and is for the sale of all goods that are not foodstuffs.

Smoking Places.—Deep-sided brass trays, fitted on stanchions and bulkheads on smoking decks, make a most remarkable difference to the cleanliness of the decks.

Matches, bits of paper, etc., are all expected to find their way into the spitkids, but on a windy day they have a way of missing the mark.

The plumber makes these trays, and they are not only useful but ornamental.

Ladder Protection.—For a small light ladder the best protection is a wood float like a target, so made that the bottom of the ladder drops inside it and the pressure of boats is taken entirely by the float, as the inboard side is against the ship's side; two lanyards keep it in place.

Track Chart for Mess Deck.—It is a great pity that the keeping of this chart has so fallen into disuse.

The lower deck do take a great interest in the movements and position of the ship, and it can so easily be kept by the midshipman who helps the navigating officer.

Awnings.—Large waist awnings are easily furled by fitting two extra side-ridge ropes and hauling out and in lines.

The awning is then furled by tricing up the side-ridge ropes and at the same time hauling forward or aft. The awning is then made a neat stow of and covered with painted canvas covers.

It only comes down for coaling.

The side-ridge ropes are necessary to trice the awning clear of deck fittings.

When spreading, the outhauls and roping are manned, and, as each cringle arrives opposite its stanchion, the earing is rove.

Awning earings are best made of chain. A spare bottom line, if it can be obtained, makes excellent earings. A long link let into these chain earings is useful for hooking a jigger to for respreading when hands are scarce.

One-inch wire guide ropes are very useful for spreading a quarter-deck awning. An eye worked in one end slips over an awning stanchion, and the other end is belayed to a deck fitting inside the awning when laid along the deck.

These guides will carry the awning over easily and clear of everything.

For head earings a good fitting is two rollers and a chain, which reeves over one roller, through the cringle, back over the other roller to a purchase. Haul out by the chain and belay, then man the purchase for final tautening.

When furling, let go the chain and let it unreeve itself.

On working Hawsers and Bollards.—Everyone has seen hawsers worked on bollards and capstans 'scientifically' in shipyards—that is to say, the right number of men backing up the right number of turns for the strength of the wire.

It is not so often seen in the service, owing to the large number of men usually available; and a not uncommon sight is a picking-up rope with a large number of turns round the capstan, backed up by half a watch of seamen.

The result usually is an endless stream of orders to stop or start the capstan, as the officer in charge thinks the strain is increasing or decreasing.

If care is taken to back up the right number of turns with the right number of men, all this form of work is greatly simplified, because the men will be unable to haul the wire off when the strain becomes greater than the wire should be subjected to, and it must be allowed to surge.

A good example of this is when using capstan and cable holder together for hauling forward slack cable. It is such easy work if the right numbers are used, and such tiresome work if orders to surge and stop and start are being given all the time.

Motor Bollards should all have a hole drilled in the outer flange. For inboard coaling whips, purchase and topping lifts of small derricks, provisioning whips, etc., no hands should be used for backing up the wires.

All these wires should have an eye worked in the end, and this eye should be rove through the hole and a toggle put through to secure it. The toggle should be secured by a small chain, otherwise it is always lost at the critical moment.

There is an impression that backing up wires by manual labour is better seamanship, but no one ever suggested it for a main derrick; and, as a rule, the brake of a main derrick motor is not so quick to act as that of a deck motor bollard.

To man the ends of inboard coaling whips is sheer waste of men.

Check Leave Boards.—These boards are fitted on the upper deck, and are a public notice of what men are on shore, sick, in detention, in cells, or under stoppage of leave.

Five boards are required—namely, seamen, stokers, marines, petty officers, and chief petty officers.

The boards are drilled with small holes to take pegs, and watch-bill numbers are painted in against the holes.

The trough at the foot of the boards is for the pegs, and these are of four colours—namely:

Red for long leave.

White for short leave.

Green for sick.

Black for detention or cells, or leave stopped.

The method of working these boards is as follows:

Liberty men fall in opposite their own boards, and, as each man is checked in the leave book, he calls his watch-bill number and the petty officer puts the red or white peg in the right hole.

When all are checked, the board is locked up and the key hung on the routine board.

Liberty men returning from leave fall in opposite their own boards, and as they are checked in the leave book, the petty officer withdraws the pegs.

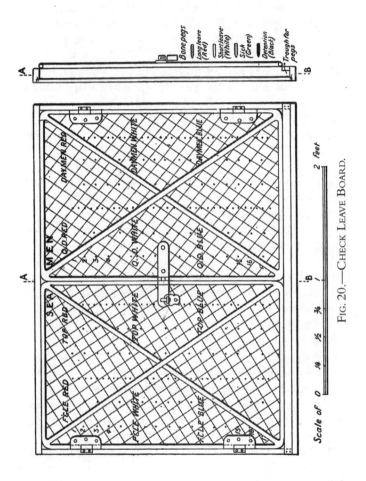

Fig. 20.—Check Leave Board.

Chief petty officers and petty officers are responsible for placing in and taking out the pegs themselves.

There is thus a public notice of everyone on shore.

The regulating staff are responsible for the pegs of men under stoppage of leave, men in detention or cells, and men on the sick list.

This scheme is of great benefit to officers and petty officers. Officers can always find out quickly if a man is on board, and can at any time quickly check the leave, if anything wrong is suspected; petty officers acting as captains of tops, or in charge of parties, can find out immediately which of their men are on shore. In a ship where these boards were in use, it was a common thing to hear an officer send a messenger to see if, for example, 'Chief Petty Officer 4' was on board or not, and petty officers were constantly going to the boards to see where their men were before falling in.

On Watertight Doors.—The captains of tops must know their doors as soon after commissioning as possible.

The method sometimes adopted is to read out to the hands the A, B, and C doors under their charge. The result is a very breathless executive officer and a ship's company little the wiser, as they have not the least idea where most of the compartments and bulkheads are.

Plans of the ship can easily be obtained or made for each captain of top; and the captains of tops should go round all the doors with the plans before any attempt is made at closing them as an evolution.

The papering of the doors with squares of paper showing the men who close the doors, is very unsatisfactory; it looks untidy, spoils an otherwise smooth enamel surface, and invariably ends in the papers tearing off.

A much better scheme, which is unmistakable and will last the whole commission and add to instead of detracting from the appearance of the between decks, is to paint the inside of the block letters different colours according to the part of the ship that closes them.

A, B, C in red are fxle men's doors.

A, B, C in white are top men's doors.

A, B, C in blue are quarter-deck men's doors.

Keeping Watertight Doors Efficient.—Difficulty is sometimes experienced in arriving at a good working scheme, as the seamen close many of the doors and the E.R. department make good defects. The following has worked well: Shipwrights are told off to inspect sections of the watertight doors at fixed intervals; any defects discovered are reported to chief carpenter, who takes a defect chit to the commander for signature; the chit is then sent to the senior engineer-lieutenant.

The shipwright who is responsible for that section reports to the carpenter as soon as the defect is made good, and the carpenter deletes the defect from his book. It is the duty of captains of tops to report to the section shipwrights any defects they may discover.

This system is a much surer one for maintaining efficiency than the common one of captains of tops reporting defects direct to O.O.D. or O.O.W. Captains of tops change, O.O.D.'s change, but the carpenter and his staff seldom change.

Fire Brigade.—The complete fire station is not nearly so important as the formation of a fire brigade.

To close the whole of the ventilation and start getting the boats out when a small fire is discovered in some out-of-the-way compartment, is analogous to calling out the whole of the London fire brigade for a small fire at a Putney villa.

An efficient fire brigade should be formed who answer a special bugle, and the complete fire station can be sounded if the fire gets a hold.

Fire Brigade.—All artisan ratings.

All lower deck and bath-room sweepers.

Torpedo men of the watch.

These men to be trained in the working of hoses, which ventilation to close, etc., for a fire in any part of the ship.

Entering Harbour.—There is nothing that looks so well or is such a good time-saver as a good evolution on entering harbour, and it is a great pity that there has been a tendency, during the last few years, to perform the various operations one after the other instead of all together. Booms, ladders, main derrick, small derricks should all move together with the bugle, and the moment hands are available the awnings should be spread. In some ships the hands are all kept waiting to spread the awnings until the main derrick has finished working, because the derrick guys work along the deck that the awning is to spread over; if the fact that a man might get his foot caught in a block is going to influence these matters, sailors will soon lose their reputation as 'handymen.'

The 'Stop everything, there's been an accident' school is not the best to bring up men-of-war's men in.

The following will make a smart evolution:

All hands fall in properly near their work.

'G.'—Man all guys, stand by ladder falls, stand by to let go anchor.

'Commence.'—Top all derricks, lower cutters, lower ladders, haul out lower and quarter booms.

'Spread awnings.'—Piped the moment the booms are out.

'Fall in.'

'Disperse.'

'Watches for exercise clear up decks, respread awnings.'

'Haul taut and coil down ropes.'

To make the evolution really smart, the commander should fall the men in again as soon as possible; the awnings may not be perfectly spread and ropes may require tautening, but fall everyone in and complete the drill and then respread, clear up, etc., with the deck hands.

Collecting Money from the Ship's Company.—This is a delicate subject, but there is no doubt that there is a right and a wrong way of collecting money for charitable objects from a ship's company.

No one would venture to lay down the law on this subject, but experience shows that:

1. Printed forms distributed round a mess deck lead to little response.

2. A collection made near the pay table on pay day, provided the captain or chaplain have fully explained the purpose for which funds are wanted, is generally very successful.

The Trafalgar Day Fund is practically the only fund that a general appeal is made for; subscriptions to other charities are usually made from the canteen funds or privately.

The reason why a 'pay-table collection' is, as a rule, successful is that it is a matter of individual action and not collective action; there are always men on a mess deck who, out of perversity, will persuade their messmates from doing what might be termed the 'right thing.'

CHAPTER XIV

LAUNDRY

The naval custom is that the junior ratings wash their own clothes and the senior ratings give their clothes out for washing when not at home ports.

The result is the formation in ships of what are known on the lower deck as 'dhobie firms,' and these consist, as a rule, of men who are employed as bath-room sweepers, men in charge of drying rooms, and in similar positions.

The prices usually charged are:

> 2*d*. per piece for clothing,
> 6*d*. for hammocks,
> 1*s*. for blankets,

and these firms do a very good business in ships with many senior ratings.

As an experiment a proper laundry was installed in one of H.M. ships, and the results are given here. (Complement about 1000)

The question of the desirability of establishing a laundry depends, of course, on the complement. It is evident from the results of this experiment that it will be a great success and make for greater cleanliness, and be a great advantage to the ship's company, at any rate in large ships.

At first sight it would appear to be an undesirable innovation as taking the washing of clothes out of the men's hands altogether; and it cannot be denied that that effect would be bad, as all men should be able to wash and look after their own clothes, blankets, and hammocks. But in practice the younger men still wash the majority of their clothes; and the laundry is of more benefit to them for washing gear so badly soiled that it probably will otherwise be thrown away, and for such difficult gear as blankets.

The senior ratings, who usually paid an exorbitant price to their own shipmates for washing, get the full benefit.

The laundry was installed by a firm of laundry manufacturers who supply plants to large passenger steamers.

It was bought by the firm contracting for the canteen, and this matter of original cost is the only difficulty that will be met with.

It is suggested as an alternative that the ship should purchase the required apparatus on a monthly instalment system. It is, of course, necessary to ascertain through the canteen committee whether the ship's company desire it.

The laundry is run by a staff of ship's ratings under the supervision of a committee of officers. A good committee is formed from the three officers of mess decks—namely, first lieutenant, engineer officer in charge of stokers' mess deck, and officer commanding marines.

Profits.—After all expenses are paid, the profits are turned over to the canteen committee for expenditure.

Staff and Organisation.—(Complement about 1000.)

The laundry is worked by one leading hand, two seamen, two stokers, and one marine. Their duties are as follows:

LAUNDRY, H.M.S. " "

Name ....

Mess ....

Date 19

No.	Articles			Rate	*s.*	*d.*
	Flannels ..	..	..	each 1*d.*		
	Drawers ..	..	..	pair 1*d.*		
	Socks	..	..	,, ½*d.*		
	Stockings ..	..	..	,, ½*d.*		
	Jean Collars	..	..	each 1*d.*		
	Handkerchiefs	..	..	,, ½*d.*		
	Serge Suits	..	..	,, 3*d.*		
	Duck Suits	..	..	,, 2*d.*		
	Canvas Suits	..	..	,, 4*d.*		
	Overalls ..	..	..	,, 4*d.*		
	Check Shirts	..	..	,, 1*d.*		
	White Shirts	..	..	,, 1*d.*		
	Soft Shirts	..	..	,, 1*d.*		
	Football Shirts	..	..	,, 1*d.*		
	Jerseys ..	..	..	,, 2*d.*		
	Sweaters ..	..	..	,, 2*d.*		
	Cholera Belts	..	..	,, 1*d.*		
	Towels ..	..	..	,, 1*d.*		
	Fearnought Trousers		..	pair 2*d.*		
	Cooks' Aprons	..		each 2*d.*		
	White Jackets	..	..	,, 1½*d.*		
	Bed Covers	..	..	,, 2*d.*		
	Pillowcases	..	..	,, 1*d.*		
	Blankets ..	..	..	,, 6*d.*		
	Sheets ..	..	..	,, 3*d.*		
	Hammocks	..	..	,, 4*d.*		
	Tablecloths	..	..	,, 6*d.*		
	Sleeping Suits	..	..	,, 3*d.*		
				Total.		

Laundry Manager ....

Clean Clothes received by ....

Date ....

Leading hand.—Washing machine and receiving clothes.

One hand.—Wringer.

One hand.—Transporting clothes to and from drying room, and drying room.

One hand.—Mangle.

Two hands.—Sorting.

Bills are made up and collected monthly by an A.B., who acts as accountant. This duty has been successfully performed by Lieutenant (G.'s) writer.

Rules.—1. The laundry will be opened for the receipt of washing from 7 A.M. until it is found that sufficient work has accumulated for the day.

2. No clothes will be received unless they are properly marked.

3. When clothes are brought to the laundry, a printed clothes' list (page 123) is brought with them.

4. When the owner wishes his clothes back, he goes to the laundry, and if his clothes are correct, signs his name at the bottom of the clothes' list as a receipt.

5. This clothes' list is then filed for entry in the account book.

6. The accounts will be made out montnly

by messes on a monthly account sheet (see attached).

LAUNDRY, H.M.S. "   "
Monthly Account Sheet
PARTICULARS FOR CATERERS OF MESSES

Mess ....   *Date* *19*

Name	Amount of 1st week	Amount of 2nd week	Amount of 3rd week	Amount of 4th week	Amount of 5th week	Month's Totals of Individuals		
				Grand Total for Mess for Month £			

7. The monthly account sheets will be given to the caterers of messes at the end of each month, and they will recover the money from individual members and hand it over to the accountant.

8. A detailed statement of accounts will be posted quarterly; accounts being audited in the usual service manner.

Note.—The printed clothes' lists can either be obtained at the laundry, or messes can obtain sheafs of these chits to keep in their messes.

Wages of Staff.—Leading hand about £2. Assistants and accountant about £1.

Special Charges for Service Washing:

	s.	d.	
Blankets .	3	0	per doz.
Counterpanes	3	6	,,
Mattress covers	2	6	,,
Pillowcases .	0	9	,,
Sheets . .	1	0	,,
Towels . .	1	3	,,

Balance Sheet.—For ten months, during which little white gear was worn and laundry was frequently closed on account of staff being required at action or night attack stations, the total receipts were £451, or an average of about £45 per month.

TYPICAL MONTHLY BALANCE SHEET

CREDITS			DEBITS		
£	s.	d.	£	s.	d.
By bills . 45	0	0	By wages. 8	0	0
			Stores:		
			2 cwt. washing		
			powder . 1	13	0
			1 cwt. soap . 1	1	0
			3 cwt. soda .	19	6
			By rent . . 10	0	0
			£21	13	6
			Profit . . 23	6	6
Total . £45	0	0	Total . £45	0	0

To this debit side must be added small bills for chalk, pencils, bills, cleaning gear, etc.

From this it will be seen that the prices, low as they are, could be still further cut down—e.g. serge suits could be 2*d*., overalls 3*d*., etc.

Profits must be accumulated to supply the necessary sum of money for purchasing spare armatures for motors and other gear likely to require renewal.

Plant Recommended for a Ship with Complement about 1000 :

> Two washing machines.
> One wringer.
> One mangle.
> Apparatus for large-sized drying room.
> Spare armatures for motors.
> Spares for machines.

Contract for a year's supply of washing materials should be made as soon as average expenditure is ascertained, as this effects a great saving.

CHAPTER XV

PAPER SHOP

The custom in the service is that the postman brings off a certain number of papers and magazines, and sells them at 'ship prices' to the ship's company.

This practice, though it comes under the heading of trafficking, is usually winked at, as the postman has to stand any loss incurred from unsold papers.

Also, in ships that are usually at ports where leave is given, the number brought off is small, as the men buy their own ashore.

But it is a very different matter when a ship is not giving leave, and the postman can easily sell twelve dozen ½d. papers a day in a ship with a complement of about 1000, even at double prices.

The usual ship prices are 1d. for ½d. papers, and 1½d. for 1d. papers, which produces a very large profit, made out of the pockets of the lower deck, which is most undesirable.

The following account of establishing a paper shop in one of H.M. ships shows what an enormous business can be developed for the benefit of the ship's company.

Paper shop was built in a suitable corner on the upper deck.

Canteen committee took over control, and agreed to pay a manager (who by reason of his experience was the postman) £1 per month and an assistant 15s. per month.

All papers, magazines, stamps, registered letter envelopes to be sold at this shop at shore prices.

Hours of Opening.—Weekdays, 11.45 to 1.0 and 5.30 to 7.0.

Sundays, after church to 12.0 and 6.0 to 7.0.

A good stock of books, novels, and monthly periodicals was always on show, and an order book was in use for men ordering special papers or regular daily papers.

Results of a typical nine days.—Papers sold each day between June 22 and 30:

PAPER SHOP

			Dailies		Periodicals
June	22	.	27½	doz.	4¼ doz.
,,	23	.	27½	,,	4 ,,
,,	24	.	36½	,,	2¼ ,,
,,	25	.	31½	,,	4½ ,,
,,	26	.	36½	,,	Sold out.
,,	27	.	42½	,,	(Sunday papers.)
,,	28	.	35½	,,	13½doz.
,,	29	.	39	,,	12½ ,,
,,	30	.	39½	,,	9½ ,,

Novels and paper-covered books and magazines, which had a good sale, are not shown in above; about one hundred per week were sold.

The canteen committee undertook to make good any losses; but with skilful management there are no losses, as the manager can soon gauge the requirements of the ship's company.

Slight profits from the discount allowed when buying large quantities of papers and periodicals go towards paying the salaries.

CHAPTER XVI

CINEMATOGRAPH

No better way of spending the canteen profits can be found than by establishing a cinematograph.

It is an endless source of amusement; and if the films are regularly changed, it can be in use two or three nights a week throughout the commission.

Machine can be bought either direct from the makers or a second-hand one obtained through a sale and exchange agency.

One of H.M. ships obtained a secondhand machine in excellent order for £6 10s.

Changing Films.—There are various film agencies, and the following are two typical arrangements:

The C. Film Agency, 4000 feet per week—i.e. about 1½ hours' performance; 10s. per week, postage paid one way.

The G. Agency, 5s. per 1000 feet of film, to be retained up to three months.

Operators.—An L.T.O. can easily look after and operate the machine. In one ship he was paid £1 per month by canteen committee; in another, service was voluntarily given.

Insurance.—It is most necessary to insure the apparatus; 30s. per cent, is a typical insurance for an expensive machine.

CHAPTER XVII

BARBER'S SHOP

There must be, in a large complement, many barbers employed, and if possible a place should be found for these men to exercise their trade.

It is much more satisfactory than having a number of men cutting hair and shaving on the mess deck.

The following statistics are given to show the trade in a ship with a complement of about 1000. Two barbers worked in the shop.

			Hair Cuts	Shaves
Wednesday.—Opened	6.0 P.M.			
Closed 10 P.M.	• • •		27	53
Thursday.—Opened	4.40 P.M.			
Closed 10 P.M.	• • •		20	47
(Shop closed from 8.50 to 9.35 for General Quarters. One barber with band from 7.0 to 9.0)				
Friday.—Opened	5.15 P.M.			
Closed 10 P.M.	• • •		22	36
(One barber with band from. 7.0 to 9.0)				
Saturday.—Opened	5.0 P.M.			
Closed 10 P.M.	• • •		22	98

These statistics are for a usual week, and are interesting as showing the desirability of establishing a proper shop for the barbers.

CHAPTER XVIII

CHAPEL

This is one of the best things that can be added to a man-of-war if space can be found.

As a rule there is some fairly large lobby space where a small chapel can be built in.

What is badly wanted is a proper place to hold communion and special services, and it is never satisfactory to put up some flags as a temporary expedient.

The ship's staff can make and fit up all the essential parts; the offertories will soon add those items which it is not possible to make on board.

There is this one thing to be avoided—the chapel is certain to be very small and on that account should not be used for any service which a fair congregation may be expected at. If this is not done, the same small coterie will attend all services to the detriment of the general spiritual tone of the ship.

CHAPTER XIX

RECREATIONS, ETC.

Gymnastic Apparatus (see pages 134-5).—In the summer, rig as much apparatus as possible on the upper deck. This can be used as an alternative to the usual drill after divisions and during the silent hours.

A plan is shown of a battle cruiser fitted out for gymnastics. The results are most gratifying, and large parties of men will be found spending the dog watches at the apparatus.

When using the apparatus for drill in the forenoon, divide up the divisions into the number of separate parties required, and use a 'G' on the bugle to move everyone on to the next apparatus.

Two exercises on the horizontal bar gives a good standard to work on.

The falling in, doubling to the next apparatus, and commencing the first exercise when the 'G' goes, must be livened up, otherwise not nearly enough exercises will be got through in the available time.

Association Football.—Start an 'interpart of the ship' league as soon as possible. Officers can present a small challenge cup to be displayed on the winning team's mess deck, and canteen committee give small medals to the winning team each year.

The ship team generally look after themselves well, and what is wanted is to start a league that will bring in *as many players as possible.*

As a rule, men who play in the ship team are excluded from their part of the ship team.

Unless a reliable man is detailed to collect the ship team's jerseys after the season, and have them washed and stowed away, they will certainly not be forthcoming the following season.

FIG. 21.—SHIP'S COMPANY AT MORNING GYMNASTICS.

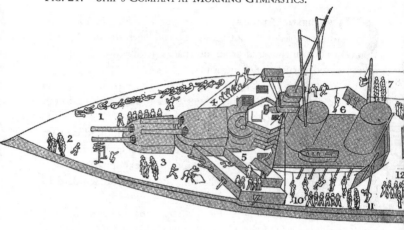

1. Tug of War.
2. Jump.
3. Buck.
4. Wall Bars.
5. Horizontal Climbing Rope.

6. Vertical Climbing Ropes.
7. Trapeze (Coaling Derrick).
8. Horse.
9. Travelling Rings (Awning Jackstay).

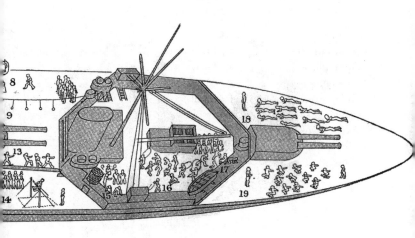

10. Vertical Climbing Ropes.
11. Rings (Coaling Derrick).
12. Parallel Bars.
13. Balancing (Coaling Derrick).
14. Horizontal Bar

15. Shelf Drill.
16. Skipping.
17. Shelf Drill.
18. Swedish Drill.
19. Swedish Drill.

Intership Assault-at-Arms.—Though seldom carried out, an intership assault-at-arms is generally a great success if the two ships are what are known as 'chummy ships,' particularly on a foreign cruise or when leave is not being given. The following events are taken from a few assaults-at-arms:

Bayonet:	*Boxing:*
Team of 10	Light heavy
Individual	Heavy
High jump	Middle
Sabres:	Light
Open	Feather
Not P.T.I.'s	Welter
Foils:	*Wrestling:*
Open	Catch weight
Not P.T.I.'s	Light weight
Tug of War:	
Catch weight	
Light weight	*Miniature rifle shooting*

The above are events when no shore grounds are available.

Subscriptions from officers and canteens to provide a challenge cup and small silver prizes for the winners.

If a football ground is available, add:

Football:
    C.P.O.'s and P.O.'s.
    Ship teams.
    Boys.

Drum And Fife Bands.—Men to play drums and fifes, if volunteers are called for, come forward in the most amazing numbers. Amongst the stokers there are always a number who have played in village bands, music hall orchestras, and even army bands.

It is a splendid thing to inaugurate in a ship, and is most useful for landing parties, etc.

The flutes are B flat flutes, and cost about 4s. each.

The drums and some of the flutes can be demanded as gunner's stores, but if the demand meets with a cold response, the canteen committee will probably fit out the band.

In a ship of complement about 1000, two bands were easily formed, one of seamen and marines and one of stokers, each playing seventeen flutes, seven side-drums, and one big drum.

Hobbies Club.—This is a club which will do a great deal of good in a ship, and be of great benefit to the men interested in fretwork, bent-iron work, mat making, repoussé work, picture framing, etc., of which there are always a large number in the complement.

The object of forming a club is to obtain goods in quantity and therefore at reduced prices, to obtain proper instruction, and to hold competitions, etc.

The following are the details of a club so formed in a ship with a complement of about 1000.

Members fifty (middle of the summer, expected to double in the winter).

Club is run on business lines, with a warrant officer as manager and a committee consisting of a secretary, treasurer, workshop manager, and storekeeper.

Capstan engine flat is used as a workshop, but any quiet compartment or flat could be used.

Members pay 2s. entrance fee and is. per month subscription, which moneys are used for prizes and to pay a small remuneration to the secretary and storekeeper.

Some very fine work can be turned out, and additional members will be always joining as they see the good results.

RULES AND REGULATIONS

1. That the Club shall be called the 'Hobbies Club.'

2. The object of the Club is to provide a pleasant and profitable pastime to members of the ship's company during leisure hours.

3. That the Club shall be governed by a Committee consisting of the following: President, Vice-President, Chairman and Treasurer, Secretary, Workshop Manager and Storekeeper, Assistant Workshop Manager and Storekeeper, Instructor, and two other members of the Club.

4. That each member shall pay an entrance of 2s. and a monthly subscription of 1s. 6d.; and that two boys be accepted into the Club as honorary members, until they attain the age of eighteen.

5. That all arrears of subscriptions be paid within three months. Any member failing to do this is liable, at the discretion of the Committee, to be expelled from the Club.

6. Five per cent, on the profit on all articles sold is to be paid into the Club funds.

7. Each member shall pay his account monthly.

In the case of single orders of £2 and over, 25 per cent, of the amount is to be paid with the order.

In the case of a series of orders which eventually total £2 or over, 25 per cent, of the amount is to be paid when the total reaches £2.

If, under special circumstances, he is unable to pay the whole of the amount owing on the first of the month, at least 75 per cent, of it is to be paid. All accounts are to be settled by the end of the quarter.

8. That all members entered after September 1 shall pay subscriptions from July 1.

9. All members are requested to attend all General Meetings.

10. Any member wishing to retire from the Club shall forfeit all claim on the Club funds.

11. Any member may use the workshop, *when off duty*, between the hours of 10 A.M. and 10 P.M.

12. A duty hand will be told off by Assistant Workshop Manager every night to clear up workshop.

13. Any tools left about the workshop after working hours will be put into store, and will be returned to owners on payment of 1d. per piece.

14. All tools borrowed from store to be returned the same evening, and members shall make good all breakages.

15. Bad language strictly prohibited. Any member infringing this rule shall place ½d. in the fine box.

16. Any member who wilfully infringes these rules is liable, at the discretion of the Committee, to be expelled from the Club.

Forming a Concert Party.—Nearly every ship has a concert party; they are probably all run on different lines, but the following notes are true for all.

It is essential to get an officer to volunteer to superintend the party.

The canteen committee should not be approached for a grant until the party have exhibited their talents; many concert parties come to grief through obtaining a grant for stage properties before they have discovered whether their efforts will be appreciated.

Only too often a party that has spent many hours practising for an entertainment, find themselves left to rig and unrig the stage themselves. The concert party is presumably started by permission of the executive officer, and therefore it is up to him to meet the requests of the officer in charge for hands to assist as far as he can; many a party has come to grief in its infancy from lack of assistance.

In the summer it is an excellent plan for the concert party to give short entertainments on the upper deck in the evening; no stage or paraphernalia, but simply a sing-song. A party that will only perform with the assistance of dresses, footlights, full orchestra, etc., is not very much good to the ship.

Organising an Upper Deck for Recreation (see pages 142-3).—Much can be done in the summer months in a large ship in the way of upper-deck recreation.

Miniature rifle shooting, roller skating, bathing, cricket, boxing, wrestling, gymnastics can all go on at once if the deck is properly divided up.

The best place for *miniature rifle shooting* is, in most ships, on the fxle. It is a very popular form of amusement, and should be run by the gunner's mates.

Matches between different sections of the ship's company are soon started when the range is in working order.

Roller Skating.—A large number of men will take up this recreation if a space can be found for them. It does little harm to the deck.

Bathing.—It is difficult to pipe 'hands to bathe' in harbours where a strong tide runs; and, in any case, bathing must be restricted to definite hours, when a boat can be in attendance.

The ordinary canvas bath is much too small to be of use for a large ship's company, but the foremost part of the fxle awning, which is rarely used, makes a splendid bath, and will take forty or fifty bathers.

When rigged in position, a drain must be cut.

If the outer side is held up by jiggers to awning stanchions, and the inner side by a wire ridge rope, the whole bath can be taken down in a few minutes.

A good routine is for the boatswain's mate of the middle watch to fill the bath before the hands turn out; the bath is emptied during 'Scrub decks' and refilled again at 'Clear up decks for quarters.'

Cricket can be organised on the upper deck of most big ships.

The seine net spread along the ship's side on stanchions or temporary spars is all that is required.

Interpart of the ship cricket matches should be played in order to spread the cricket over as many men as possible.

Gymnastic Gear should be rigged in the dog watches as previously described.

Boxing and Wrestling will have many followers if a place is told off for these pursuits.

Sports Depot.—Every officer who has 'run' football teams, cricket teams, regattas, etc., in a man-of-war knows the difficulties of looking after the jerseys, footballs, bats, etc.

As a rule, the canteen committee vote considerable sums of money for sports gear, and little can be traced when the different sports recommence after an interval. It is no unusual thing to see the ship's colours in a collier's hold, and a pump for blowing up footballs is never at hand.

All difficulties can be avoided by adopting proper business methods.

A small compartment should be set aside for the stowage of all sports gear, and a yeoman appointed to look after the store.

A lower deck sweeper, gunnery officer's writer, sailmaker's mate, or any man in semi-excused employment, makes a good yeoman.

He keeps an issue book, and opens the store at all times of departure from the ship or arrival from the shore of recreation parties.

He is responsible for the good order and cleanliness of the gear.

As this system ensures no unnecessary wastage, the canteen committee will probably be prepared to stock this depot with sufficient jerseys for all teams and a proportion over and above the actual requirements to allow of regular washing.

A proper check is kept on all gear, and worn-out gear replaced by the committee.

Benefit Societies.—Many ships now form benefit societies, and the following rules, which proved successful in one of H.M. ships, may be useful as a guide:

RULES OF THE '——BENEVOLENT SOCIETY'

1. That this Society be called the '——Benevolent Society.'

2. That there be a President, Vice-President, Honorary Treasurer and Secretary.

3. That the working of the Society, according to the established rules, be ordered and supervised by a Committee, of which the President, Vice-President, and Secretary will be *ex-officio* members, the remaining members of the Committee to be elected every six months, the former members being eligible for re-election. Four members of the Committee and the Secretary, in addition to either the President or Vice-President, shall form a quorum. The Honorary Treasurer shall not be eligible to sit on the Committee.

4. The Elective Committee shall consist of the following:

> One chief petty officer.
> Two petty officers.
> One leading seaman.
> Two able seamen.
> One dayman rating.
> One band rating.
> One E.R.A. or electrical artificer.
> One mechanician or chief stoker.
> One stoker petty officer.
> One leading stoker.
> One stoker.
> One royal marine.

FIG. 22.—Upper Deck Recreation.

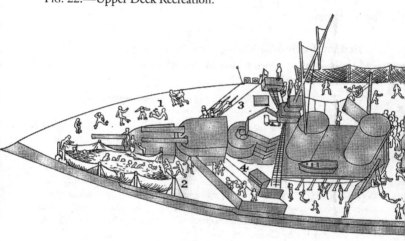

1. Roller Skating
2. Large Swimming Bath (Fxle Awning).

3. Morris Tube Range.
4. Boxing

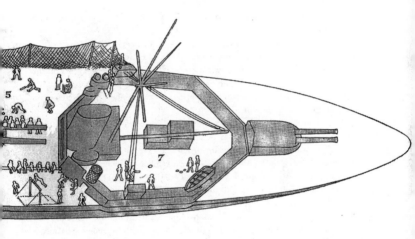

5. Cricket.

6. Gymnastics, Bayonet Fighting, etc

7. Officers. Quoits, etc

5. Whilst the Committee and the Treasurer will take every precaution and care possible, it is to be understood that they will not be individually or collectively responsible for losses occasioned by matters beyond their control, such as insolvency of bank, losses by fire, wreck or war, etc.

6. All directions to the Honorary Treasurer as to disposal of money or payments, are to be given to him in writing under the signatures of the President or the Vice-President and the Secretary, and a copy of such directions are to be laid before the Committee at their next meeting for confirmation, or for information if previously ordered by the Committee.

7. That the subscription be 6d. per month, commencing November 1, 1913, to be deducted from monthly pay bi-monthly. All boys to be honorary members until advanced to men's ratings.

8. That each member have a book of rules, which shall be purchasable from the Secretary.

9. That the Secretary shall keep a register with the names and addresses of the persons to whom members wish payment to be made in the event of death.

10. That as far as the funds allow, a sum of £2 for every 100 membsrs on the register be paid in the event of death or invaliding. If the funds do not admit of full payment, the Committee to obtain the opinions of the members they represent, in writing, as to a levy to raise the deficit.

11. That at the end of the commission, the balance remaining to the Society's credit shall be divided among the members.

12. Men who join the Society in November 1913, shall be at once entitled to full benefits. Men on the ship's books on November 1, 1913, who wish to join later, shall pay arrears as from November 1, 1913. Men who join the ship later in the commission shall be entitled to full benefits on the payment of four monthly subscriptions if they join in the first year, and six monthly subscriptions if they join after the first year, which may be paid in one sum if desired; but these men shall only receive a share proportionate to the length of their membership when the balance is distributed at the end of the commission.

13. Members ordered to another ship or 'invalided through their own fault,' shall be entitled to the return of their subscriptions after a deduction has been made for the amounts previously paid by the Society: the deductions to be determined by the Committee. Members who leave the Society of their own will shall forfeit their subscriptions.

14. The books shall be audited once in each quarter by two members not on the Committee, and a balance sheet shall be produced at a General Meeting.

15. That no rule shall be altered except at a full Committee Meeting, each member of the Committee producing the votes in writing of the members he represents, and it shall be necessary for 75 per cent. of the members on the register to be in favour of the alteration.

Fourteen days' clear notice must be given to the Secretary, in writing, of a proposed alteration in the rules, and the alteration to be posted at least seven days.

16. That boys may receive such sum as the Committee may decide, not exceeding half benefits, in case of invaliding if due to other than their own fault.

17. That no man may join the Society after February 1, 1914, unless approved by the Committee.

18. Any member wishing to cease membership must give notice to the Secretary in writing.

OFFICERS' RECREATIONS ON BOARD SHIP

The following notes may prove useful.

BILLIARD TABLE.—The movements of a modern big ship are so slight when at anchor that billiard balls will run with accuracy.

A miniature billiard table is a great asset in a mess, particularly in the winter. These miniature tables are sold in various sizes: 8 feet 4 inches by 4 feet 4 inches is a good size for a mess, and costs about £12.

If a small charge is made a table soon pays for itself.

These tables are supplied with adjustable feet, but large brass screw feet for the table legs can easily be made on board and are preferable.

If desired, most firms will arrange for payment by monthly instalments, which add about 5 per cent, to cost price.

MEDICINE BALL.—These balls cost about 12s., and plenty of hard exercise can be obtained with them.

If a miniature tennis court is chalked out on the deck and a piece of spun yarn used for a net, a game played with this ball under lawn tennis rules provides splendid exercise.

SQUASH COURT.—An excellent squash court can be made as follows:

Front wall is formed from a screen or engine-room casing heightened by plates if necessary.

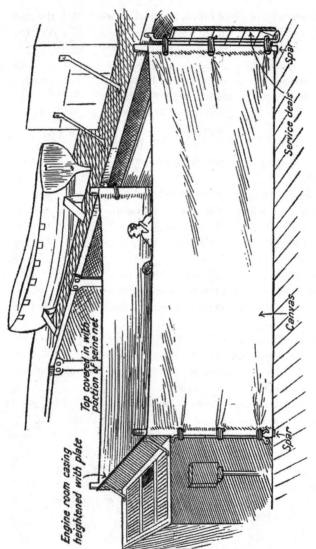

Top covered in with
portion of seine net

Engine room casing
heightened with plate

Service deals

Spar

Canvas

Spar

Fig. 23.—Squash Court.

Side walls are made of canvas and pockets are sewn in the ends to take spars; the benefit of reeving these spars is that very few lashings are required to rig, unrig, or retauten the sides.

The back wall is made of ordinary deals placed one on top of the other. About 15 feet 6 inches is a good width to make the court, as the 16-feet service deals are then ready to hand.

Such a court is in use in one of H.M. ships, and can be rigged and unrigged in about ten minutes.

When unrigging, the sides are rolled up and the deals, which are held in place by a bar, are 'unrove' and stowed in their usual stowage.

A piece of the seine net is used to cover in the top.

A ball hit straight at canvas will drop dead, but a ball striking at an angle will 'come off' quite well, and the slowing up which occurs when the ball hits the side walls is an advantage when the court is short.

The game can be played either with tennis rackets and tennis ball or squash rackets and white indiarubber ball; it is probably necessary to keep the front wall grey, so a black ball is difficult to use.

The canvas for side walls should be painted the necessary colour with distemper in order to keep the canvas flexible for rolling up and also to keep its original dimensions.

INDEX

The Pool of London Press is a publisher inspired by the rich history and resonance of the stretch of the River Thames from London Bridge downriver to Greenwich. The Press is dedicated to the specialist fields of naval, maritime, military and exploration history in its many forms. The fine history of London and the Thames also features. The Press produces beautifully designed, commercial, non-fiction volumes and digital products of outstanding quality for a dedicated readership featuring strong narratives, magnificent illustrations and the finest photography.

A selection of titles from the Pool of London Press can be found on the following pages.

POOLOFLONDON
WWW.POOLOFLONDON.COM

THE COLD WAR SPY POCKET-MANUAL

The Official Field-manuals for Spycraft, Espionage and Counter-intelligence

Edited and compiled by Philip Parker

Some twenty-five years after its conclusion, yet with its echoes resonating once more in contemporary East-West relations, the rigors and detail of many aspects of the Cold War are becoming increasingly of interest. Furthermore, at the very same time many of the records of the period are beginning to become accessible for the first time. At the forefront of this unique conflict, that divided the world into two opposing camps for over four decades, were the security services and the agents of these secretive organizations.

The Cold War Spy Pocket-Manual presents a meticulously compiled selection of recently unclassified documents, field-manuals, briefing directives and intelligence primers that uncover the training and techniques required to function as a spy in the darkest periods of modern history. Material has been researched from the CIA, MI6, the KGB and the STASI. As insightful as any drama these documents detail, amongst many other things, the directives that informed nuclear espionage, assassinations, interrogations and the 'turning' and defection of agents.

- Full introduction and commentary provided by leading historian and former diplomat.

- Presents for the first time the insightful documents, many of which inspired Cold War novelists including John Le Carré, Len Deighton and Ian Fleming.

- Beautifully retro-styled and cloth-bound.

£8.99 • Hardback • 128 pages • ISBN 978-1-910860-02-1

THE LAST BIG GUN

At War & At Sea with HMS *Belfast*

Brian Lavery

As she lay in dry dock, devastatingly damaged by one of Hitler's newly deployed magnetic mines after barely two months in service, few could have predicted the illustrious career that lay ahead for the cruiser HMS *Belfast*. After three years of repairs to her broken keel, engine- and boiler-rooms, and extensive refitting, she would go on to play a critical role in the protection of the Arctic Convoys, would fire one of the opening shots at D-Day and continue supporting the Operation Overlord landings for five weeks.

Her service continued beyond the Second World War both in Korea and in the Far East before she commenced her life as one of the world's most celebrated preserved visitor ships in the Pool of London. Her crowning glory however came in December 1943 when, equipped with the latest radar technology, she was to play the leading role in the Battle of the North Cape sinking the feared German battlecruiser *Scharnhorst*, the bête-noir of the Royal Navy. In doing so the ship's crew made a vital contribution to, what was to be, the final big-gun head-to-head action to be fought at sea.

In *The Last Big Gun* Brian Lavery, the foremost historian of the Royal Navy, employs his trademark wide-ranging narrative style and uses the microcosm of the ship to tell the wider story of the naval war at sea and vividly portray the realities for all of life aboard a Second World War battleship.

- The illustrious survivor of the last big-gun head-to-head 'broadside' engagement at sea.

- The very first complete 'biography' of HMS *Belfast*.

- Exhaustively researched from primary sources and interviews and written in the matchless narrative style of the award-winning, *Sunday Times* bestselling author Brian Lavery.

£25.00 • Hardback • 376 pages • ISBN 978-1-910860-01-4

THE MAPMAKERS' WORLD

A Cultural History of the European World Map

Marjo T. Nurminen

The Mapmakers' World illuminates the fascinating cultural history of European world maps: what do historical world maps tell of us, of our perception of the world, and of places and peoples that are foreign to us? Who were the makers of these early world maps? How were the maps created and for whom were they drawn and printed? For what purposes were they used? What kind of information did they pass on? The answers to these questions open up a fascinating narrative of discovery and cartography relating not only to ideology and political power but also the histories of art and science.

- Lavishly illustrated history of the European world map.

- One thousand years of art, science, exploration, power and propaganda.

- Great illustrations of maps, paintings and artworks from the finest private and public collections as well as specially commissioned diagrams.

- The comprehensive history of European maps in one volume telling the exciting story of how cartographers first fully imaged the globe.

£50.00 • Hardback • 360 pages • ISBN 978-1-910860-00-7